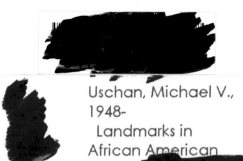

Uschan, Michael V.,
1948-
  Landmarks in
African American
history

# Landmarks in African American History

## Lucent Library of Black History

Michael V. Uschan

**LUCENT BOOKS**

*A part of Gale, Cengage Learning*

GALE
CENGAGE Learning™

Detroit • New York • San Francisco • New Haven, Conn • Waterville, Maine • London

LIBRARY OF CONGRESS CATALOGING-IN-PUBLICATION DATA

Uschan, Michael V., 1948-
  Landmarks in African American history / by Michael V. Uschan.
    p. cm. -- (Lucent library of Black history)
  Includes bibliographical references and index.
  ISBN 978-1-4205-0921-2 (hardcover)
  1. African Americans--History--Sources. 2. African Americans--Historiography.
3. African Americans--Monuments. 4. Historic sites--United States. 5. Historic
buildings--United States. 6. Monuments--United States. 7. United States--
History--Civil War, 1861-1865--Battlefields. I. Title.
  E185.U77 2012
  973'.0496073--dc23
                                                                    2012028722

Lucent Books
27500 Drake Rd.
Farmington Hills, MI 48331


ISBN-13: 978-1-4205-0921-2
ISBN-10: 1-4205-0921-7

Printed in the United States of America
1 2 3 4 5 6 7 16 15 14 13 12

# Contents

# Foreword

It has been more than 500 years since Africans were first brought to the New World in shackles, and over 140 years since slavery was formally abolished in the United States. Over 50 years have passed since the fallacy of "separate but equal" was obliterated in the American courts, and some 40 years since the watershed Civil Rights Act of 1964 guaranteed the rights and liberties of all Americans, especially those of color. Over time, these changes have become celebrated landmarks in American history. In the twenty-first century, African American men and women are politicians, judges, diplomats, professors, deans, doctors, artists, athletes, business owners, and home owners. For many, the scars of the past have melted away in the opportunities that have been found in contemporary society. Observers such as Peter N. Kirsanow, who sits on the U.S. Commission of Civil Rights, point to these accomplishments and conclude, "The growing black middle class may be viewed as proof that most of the civil rights battles have been won."

In spite of these legal victories, however, prejudice and inequality have persisted in American society. In 2003, African Americans comprised just 12 percent of the nation's population, yet accounted for 44 percent of its prison inmates and 24 percent of its poor. Racially motivated hate crimes continue to appear on the pages of major newspapers in many American cities. Furthermore, many African Americans still experience either overt or muted racism in their daily lives. A 1996 study undertaken by Professor Nancy Krieger of the Harvard School of Public Health, for example, found that 80 percent of the African American participants reported having experienced racial discrimination in one or more settings, including at work or school, applying for housing and medical care, from the police or in the courts, and on the street or in a public setting.

It is for these reasons that many believe the struggle for racial equality and justice is far from over. These episodes of dis-

crimination threaten to shatter the illusion that America has completely overcome its racist past, causing many black Americans to
become increasingly frustrated and confused. Scholar and writer
Ellis Cose has described this splintered state in the following way:
"I have done everything I was supposed to do. I have stayed out
of trouble with the law, gone to the right schools, and worked
myself nearly to death. What more do they want? Why in God's
name won't they accept me as a full human being?" For Cose and
others, the struggle for equality and justice has yet to be fully
achieved.

In many subtle yet important ways the traumatic experiences
of slavery and segregation continue to inform the way race is dis-
cussed and experienced in the twenty-first century. Indeed, it is
possible that America will always grapple with the fallout from
its distressing past. Ulric Haynes, dean of the Hofstra University
School of Business, has said, "Perhaps race will always matter,
given the historical circumstances under which we came to this
country." But studying this past and understanding how it con-
tributes to present-day dialogues about race and history in America is a critical component of contemporary education. To this
end, the Lucent Library of Black History offers a thorough look
at the experiences that have shaped the black community and the
American people as a whole. Annotated bibliographies provide
readers with ideas for further research, while fully documented
primary and secondary source quotations enhance the text. Each
book in the series explores a different episode of black history;
together they provide students with a wealth of information as
well as launching points for further study and discussion.

# Introduction

# The Importance of Landmarks

On February 22, 2012, President Barack Obama participated in the ground-breaking ceremony for the National Museum of African American History and Culture in Washington, D.C. The museum documents the long, troubled, yet triumphant history of African Americans since the first of them arrived as slaves in 1619 in the English colony of Virginia. Displays in the museum range from slave shackles small enough for a child to the trumpet musician Louis Armstrong blew so gloriously to entertain millions of people. Even the museum's location is symbolic of black history. Although its site on the National Mall is close to where a slave market once existed, it is just 1 mile (1.6km) from where Martin Luther King Jr. spoke to an estimated quarter of a million people on August 28, 1963, in a historic civil rights rally. The museum is also just a few miles distant from the White House occupied by Obama, the first African American president.

Obama and First Lady Michelle Obama were living symbols at the ground breaking of the upward path African Americans have traveled in U.S. history—from slavery to holding and wielding the power of the nation's highest office. Obama called the ceremony "a celebration of life" and said the museum was important because it would keep alive the history of African Americans: "It is on this spot—alongside the monuments to those who gave birth to this nation, and those who worked so hard to perfect it—that generations will remember the sometimes difficult, often inspirational, but always central role that African Americans have played in the life of our country."[1]

Historic landmarks clustered near the museum include monuments honoring King, presidents George Washington and Thomas Jefferson, and the soldiers who fought in World War II and the Vietnam War. Because of its importance in telling the four-century-long story of African Americans, the museum instantly became one of the nation's most important African American landmarks. However, it is only one of hundreds of landmarks spread across the length and breadth of the nation that detail the history of African Americans since before the United States even came into existence.

## Why Landmarks Are Important

Landmarks detail and memorialize the lives, tragedies, and triumphs of African Americans. They honor individuals like King, as well as events like the 1739 Stono River Slave Rebellion in South Carolina. These landmarks include parks, battlefields, museums, graves, statues, plaques, and private homes in which famous blacks once lived. Entire sections of some communities are considered landmarks, like the Sweet Auburn area in Atlanta, an early residential area for freed slaves. National, state, or local governments have officially designated many landmarks as historic sites. Yet even the loneliest grave or the smallest plaque installed by a local group is still an important symbol of African American history.

Some landmarks like the Old Slave Mart in Charleston, South Carolina, tell the tragic story of the days of slavery. Many more, however, celebrate black achievements, such as the statue in Boston of Phillis Wheatley, a former slave who was the first black to publish poetry; and the Oberlin, Ohio, home once owned by John Mercer Langston, who in 1855 became the first African American elected official. And Beckwourth, California, was named after James Pierson Beckwourth, a freed slave who went west as a fur trapper and discovered Beckwourth Pass, a trail over the Sierra Nevada that pioneers used to travel into California.

These African American landmarks are all important for several reasons. One is that they express the views of a community,

7

state, or even an entire nation about the character, values, and morality of the people or events they honor. Thomas Carlyle was a famous nineteenth-century historian and writer from Scotland. In a pamphlet in which he opposed erecting a statue to honor controversial English political leader Oliver Cromwell, Carlyle explained why statues and other landmarks are meaningful: "Show me the man you honor; I know by that symptom, better than by any other, what kind of man you yourself are. For you show me there what your ideal of manhood is; what kind of man you long inexpressibly to be."[2]

A second reason historic landmarks are important is that they need the consent of public officials because most of them are

President Obama speaks during the ground-breaking ceremonies for the National Museum of African American History and Culture in Washington, D.C. He said the museum was important because it would keep alive the history of African Americans.

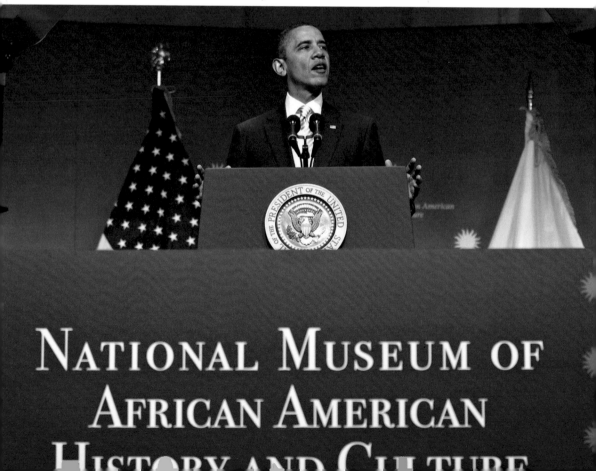

NATIONAL MUSEUM OF
AFRICAN AMERICAN
HISTORY AND CULTURE

placed in public spaces like the National Mall in Washington. Consequently, such landmarks not only honor people and their achievements but are also a form of public approval of what these people did and the ideals that motivated them.

In his first inaugural address on February 4, 1861, President Abraham Lincoln voiced another reason why public landmarks are important. After Lincoln was elected, southern states began seceding from the Union because they feared he would abolish slavery. In his appeal to those states not to divide the United States, Lincoln said southerners needed to remember the long history northern and southern states had shared since the nation was created nearly a century earlier after winning independence from England. He said: "We are not enemies, but friends. We must not be enemies. Though passion may have strained it must not break our bonds of affection. The mystic chords of memory, stretching from every battlefield and patriot grave to every living heart and hearthstone all over this broad land, will yet swell the chorus of the Union, when again touched, as surely they will be, by the better angels of our nature."[3]

The phrase "mystic chords of memory" referred to the many historic landmarks that represented the history the states had shared. Such landmarks, including those from the tragic Civil War that began soon after Lincoln's speech, today still help bind Americans together. They remind citizens of their shared history and the fact that it has taken many people from every part of the nation to create what the United States has become today.

## "The Whole Story"

U.S. representative John Lewis of Georgia was key in creating the National Museum of African American History and Culture. Lewis fought for fifteen years to have Congress approve the museum because he felt it was important to have a landmark that would forever detail the entire history of African Americans. At the ground breaking for the museum, the legendary civil rights leader said, "We must tell the story, the whole story, a 400-year story of African Americans' contributions to this nation's history from slavery to the present—without anger or apology."[4] And that is exactly what the museum and thousands of other African American landmarks have been doing for many years.

# Chapter One

# The Slavery Era

The Cape Coast Castle in Ghana, located on coast of the Atlantic Ocean in Cape Coast, is a huge, fortress-like structure with towering, whitewashed walls. It was built by Europeans, who used it from the sixteenth to the eighteenth centuries for commercial trade with Africa. Cape Coast Castle, which the United Nations Educational, Scientific and Cultural Organization has designated a World Heritage Site, is one of the most dramatic and tragic landmarks linked to the U.S. slavery era. After African men, women, and children had been kidnapped from their homes, they were held in Cape Coast Castle until they could be transported to North America to be sold as slaves. A plaque at the doorway to the dark, dim, underground dungeon in which they were imprisoned reads: "In everlasting memory of the anguish of our ancestors. May those who died rest in peace. May those who return find their roots. May humanity never again perpetuate such injustice against humanity. We, the living, vow to uphold this."[5]

Thousands of people visit Cape Coast Castle and its museum each year to see firsthand one of the most horrible landmarks of slavery and, in the case of African Americans, to better understand what happened to their ancestors. In July 2009 President Barack Obama and First Lady Michelle Obama, whose ancestors were slaves, and their daughters Malia and Sasha were among those visitors. One of the most poignant moments the Obamas experienced was to walk through the "door of no return," the prison exit through which Africans were led in chains to ships that took them away forever from their homelands. After the tour Barack Obama said: "It is reminiscent of the trip I took to Buchenwald [a Nazi concentration camp] because it reminds us of the capacity of human beings to commit great evil. . . . As African Americans, obviously there's a special sense that on the one hand this place was a place of profound sadness [because] it is here where the journey of much of the African American experience began."[6] That journey in the holds of slave ships marked the beginning of a lifetime of misery for millions of African Americans.

## The Start of Slavery

In 1607 British settlers established Virginia, the first of thirteen colonies that would one day become the United States of America. A dozen years later, in August 1619, the Dutch ship *White Lion* arrived at Virginia's port city of Virginia near present-day Hampton,

Ghana's infamous Cape Coast Castle held kidnapped Africans awaiting transport to North America as slaves.

Virginia. John Rolfe, the colony's treasurer, wrote that the ship had "brought not any thing but 20 and odd Negroes, [which were] bought for victuale [food] at the best and easyest rate they could."[7] The ship's captain sold the Africans in exchange for food. The slaves were valuable to the struggling colony because it did not have many residents and needed cheap labor to help grow tobacco, its main cash crop.

The story of how the first African American slaves arrived is part of the history detailed in Colonial National Historical Park, a National Park Service site that is near where the first slave ship docked. The park provided visitors with few details about those first African American slaves until 2006, when the park's museum added more information about them as part of its commemoration of the four hundredth anniversary of the colony's founding. One new fact is that one of the African Americans was named An-

This brick foundation is all that is left of the original Jamestown, Virginia, landing dock where slaves were unloaded after their sea voyage from Africa.

gela. The historic park's museum included a portrayal of Angela in a new film it produced about Jamestown. The historic site also honors African Americans by having historian Jerome Bridges portray slaves like Anthony Johnson, who arrived in Jamestown in the early seventeenth century. When Johnson was freed, he married, bought a farm, and even purchased indentured servants as workers.

Dressed in period costume, Bridges educates visitors about slavery and explains to them that the first African Americans were sold as indentured servants, a form of temporary slavery. This economic bondage lasted for a set number of years, usually five to seven, after which the indentured servants were freed. Thousands of white Europeans too poor to afford passage to the colonies willingly sold themselves as indentured servants. They did so because they believed they would be able to better themselves economically in the colonies once their servitude ended. But blacks were unwilling immigrants who had no choice about being taken from their homes to be sold into servitude in a strange land, no matter how long it lasted.

Bridges also tells visitors that whites and freed blacks lived together as equals for a short time after the colony started: "For one brief shining moment, there was the opportunity for Negroes to live on the same plane [as whites]. There were no slave laws. Negroes could own land. They could have indentured servants."[8] But by 1660 Virginians and people in other colonies were buying Africans as slaves for life because they provided cheap labor that benefited slave owners economically. Massachusetts in 1641 was the first colony to legalize slavery, and other colonies soon followed suit, creating a form of slavery that would not be extinguished until the end of the Civil War in 1865.

## Slave Life

For more than two centuries, Africans who arrived in the British colonies and later the United States were sold to the highest bidder at auctions; when people bought them, they could do anything they wanted with them because slaves had no rights. A marker in downtown Richmond, Virginia, is one of many historic sites linked to slave sales. The marker notes that slaves were sold at the St. Charles Hotel, which once stood near the marker.

British author William Makepeace Thackeray viewed a slave auction in Richmond on March 3, 1853. The slaves he described included a young woman holding a baby. Thackeray wrote about what happened when the auction ended: "After these sales we saw the usual exodus of negro slaves, marched under escort of their new owners across the town to the railway station, where they took places, and 'went South [to other states].' They held scanty bundles of clothing, their only possession."[9]

The vast majority of slaves lived in the South, but slavery also existed in northern colonies. Slave ships regularly landed in New Jersey, and the Quakers who first settled there bought Africans to work on their farms and businesses. Colonial cities like New York and Philadelphia had many slaves. New York's population in 1711 was only about sixty-four hundred, but nearly one thousand residents were black; almost all African Americans living there then were slaves, and an estimated 40 percent of white families owned slaves. The African Burial Ground in Manhattan, which once served as a cemetery for New York slaves, was dedicated on February 27, 2006, as a National Historic Landmark.

The number of African American slaves increased dramatically after they first arrived in Jamestown. After winning its freedom against Great Britain in the American Revolution, the new nation allowed slavery to continue even though colonists in their Declaration of Independence in 1776 had claimed they started the war because they believed that "all men are created equal."[10] The first federal census in 1790 showed there were 697,681 slaves in the United States, but by 1810 that number had risen to 1.2 million, and by 1860 there were nearly 4 million slaves. Virginia had the most slaves—292,627 in 1790 and 490,865 in 1860—but Georgia, South Carolina, and North Carolina also had huge slave populations.

On March 29, 2001, South Carolina dedicated its African-American History Monument in Columbia, the state's capital. It is the only such landmark on the grounds of a state capitol. The towering work of granite and bronze created by artist Ed Dwight is two stories high and 25 feet (7.6m) wide. The monument includes twelve panels that depict scenes that detail slave life. One panel has scenes of the Middle Passage, the brutal sea voyages that brought Africans to the shores of this country; another is of a woman and child on a slave auction block; and a third shows slaves working

Figures depicting an enslaved African family burying their dead are exhibited at New York City's African Burial Ground Museum.

at various tasks. However, the monument includes positive scenes about African American history, including imagery of South Carolina blacks who fought for their freedom in the Civil War and for their civil rights during protests in the 1950s and 1960s.

Dwight said he was excited to create panels about slave life because he wants to make sure people never forget the injustice of slavery: "Getting into [the] mechanisms of slavery is something that is so moving. You want to get up on a top of a mountain and start screaming and hollering and telling people all this stuff."[11] His stunning art will do just that for future generations who view the monument.

The slavery era lasted from 1619 until the end of the Civil War in 1865. Not all blacks in this dark period of U.S. history were slaves, and there are many landmarks that showcase the accomplishments of free blacks as well as those of African Americans who were slaves. One thing both free and enslaved blacks did was help the colonies win their independence from Great Britain.

# Founder of Chicago

The first non–Native American who lived in Chicago was an African American. Jean Baptist DuSable was born in Haiti around 1745; his father was a French sailor and his mother was black. Twenty years later he moved to Louisiana, then a French possession, and became a fur trapper who traveled up the Mississippi River. In the 1770s he established a farm and fur trading post in what would one day become Chicago. His home on the north bank of the Chicago River at its junction with Lake Michigan was the first permanent residence in Chicago. DuSable's home included buildings that housed dairy cows, chickens, horses, and a mill. During the American Revolution, DuSable supported the Americans against the British. In 1796 DuSable sold

his Chicago home and went to live with his son in St. Charles, Illinois, where he died in 1814. On May 11, 1976, the original site of his home in downtown Chicago was designated a National Historic Landmark. A plaque near the Michigan Avenue Bridge marks the site. In 2010 the bridge was renamed DuSable Bridge in his honor. Located nearby is Pioneer Court, which includes a bust of DuSable.

A bust of Jean-Baptiste DuSable commemorates the African American founder of Chicago.

## Black Patriots

Crispus Attucks was born a slave in 1722 in Framingham, Massachusetts. He escaped from his owner in 1750 and died a hero on March 5, 1770, when he was one of five men shot to death by British soldiers during the Boston Massacre. Attucks was one of a large group of men protesting an incident in which a British soldier had struck a child. The crowd was so huge and angry that British soldiers, fearing for their lives, opened fire on the protesters. Attucks was the first one killed by their gunfire. The famous historical incident was one of the earliest instances of rebellion against British rule that eventually led to the American Revolution and creation of the United States.

The five men who died are still honored today for standing up for the rights of colonists, especially Attucks, who has been called "the first to die, the first to defy [the British]."[12] Attucks biographer James Neyland wrote about his historical importance: "He is one of the most important figures in African-American history, not for what he did for his own race but for what he did for all oppressed people everywhere. He is a reminder that the African-American heritage is not only African but American and it is a heritage that begins with the beginning of America."[13]

In 1888 the Crispus Attucks Monument was erected on the Boston Common. Although it is named after Attucks, it also honors the other victims—Samuel Maverick, James Caldwell, Samuel Gray, and Patrick Carr. The towering stone monument that bears their names features a sculpture representing the Spirit of the Revolution. There is also a plaque at the actual site of the massacre that honors the slain protesters.

Another important black landmark associated with the Revolution is the Fraunces Tavern Museum in New York. In 1762 Samuel Fraunces, a West Indian of African and French parentage who was born free, purchased the tavern. The tavern became a meeting place for colonists who opposed British rule and were plotting revolution. When the Americans won the war in 1783, the tavern was the site for negotiations between American and British officials to end the seven-year occupation of New York City. Fraunces also hosted a dinner on November 25 to celebrate the British leaving the city. In 1904 the Sons of the Revolution bought the tavern, and three years later opened it as the Fraunces

Tavern Museum, which today still features exhibits on revolutionary history.

At the time of the revolution, about five hundred thousand African Americans, one-fifth the population of the colonies, were slaves, and there were an estimated forty thousand free blacks. About five thousand African Americans fought in the Continental army during the American Revolution, including many slaves who earned their freedom by joining the army. Jeff Liberty and thirty other African American soldiers are buried in Judea Cemetery in Washington, Connecticut; their gravesite has a marker that reads, "Jeff Liberty and his colored patriots."[14]

Free blacks like John Chavis of North Carolina also fought. Chavis was a soldier for three years in the Fifth Virginia Regiment. After the war, Chavis became a Presbyterian minister and a teacher in Raleigh who taught both black and white students. But in 1832 Chavis, as well as other blacks in Virginia, lost the right to preach or teach when the Virginia General Assembly passed a law prohibiting blacks from performing either task. The law was designed to punish blacks because of a slave uprising the year before led by Nat Turner. Chavis countered the offensive law by proudly declaring, "Tell them that [I] am [a] free born American and a revolutionary soldier."[15] In addition to landmarks for individual black Revolutionary soldiers, there are many honoring black military units. The First Rhode Island Regiment had so many slaves and freed black men that it was called the "Black Regiment." They fought well in the Battle of Rhode Island, on August 29, 1778, and in 2005 a plaque honoring them was dedicated in Portsmouth, Rhode Island. The site is now a National Historic Landmark.

## African American Achievements

African Americans were successful in many different endeavors during the slave period (1619–1865). Amos Fortune was born in Africa in 1710 but was kidnapped and taken to the colony of Massachusetts, where tanner Ichabod Richardson bought him and taught him how to tan hides. Richardson was one of the slave owners who was kind enough to pay skilled workers like Fortune for their work. By 1770 Fortune had saved enough of his pay to purchase his freedom. He moved to Jaffrey, New Hampshire, where he became a successful tanner who hired black and

This monument on Boston Common commemorates African American Crispus Attucks and the other victims of the Boston Massacre.

white apprentices. Fortune founded the local library and when he died left money to the school system; the Amos Fortune fund today still pays for educational activities like speaking contests. His home and barn are local historical landmarks, and he and his wife are buried in Jaffrey.

James Pierson Beckwourth was born a slave in Virginia in either 1798 or 1800 to Jennings Beckwith, an English nobleman,

# First Elected Official

On April 2, 1855, John Mercer Langston became the first African American elected to public office when he was elected town clerk of Brownhelm, Ohio. Langston was popular enough to win the position even though blacks could not vote in Ohio elections. Langston was also elected to the Oberlin, Ohio, Board of Education and the U.S. House of Representatives from Virginia and appointed U.S. minister to Haiti. Langston was born December 14, 1829, in Louisa County, Virginia, to white plantation owner Ralph Quarles; Langston's mother, Lucy Langston, was a slave Quarles had freed. Langston graduated from Oberlin College and became a lawyer. In addition to winning elective office, Langston was prominent in the fight to abolish slavery and was a noted educator as the first dean of Howard University's law school. On May 15, 1975, his home in Oberlin, Ohio, was named a National Historic Landmark. Langston once said that po-

litical power was the only way blacks could achieve equality with whites: "What we so much need [is] political influence, the bridle by which we can check and guide, to our advantage, the selfishness of American [racist] demagogues."

Quoted in Leon F. Litwack and August Meier. *Black Leaders of the Nineteenth Century*. Champaign: University of Illinois Press, 1991, p. 110.

The Ohio home of John Mercer Langston, the first African American elected to public office, was made a National Historic Landmark in 1975.

and a slave Beckwith owned. His father freed Beckwourth when he was an adult, and in 1824 he went west to trap beaver in the Rocky Mountains. Beckwourth became one of the most famous mountain men in the trapping era that lasted for nearly two decades.

Beckwourth was one of many trappers who discovered trails pioneers used to settle the West, including the states of California, Oregon, and Washington. In 1850 Beckwourth was prospecting for gold when he saw a pass in the Sierra Nevada that he reported "seemed lower than any other" and "would afford the best wagon-road into the American Valley [in California] approaching from the eastward."[16] The trail cut the route to the valley by about 150 miles (241km) from the older California Trail and was easier because it eliminated several steep grades and dangerous passes. Beckwourth, who died on October 29, 1866, in Denver, has been honored in many ways. In addition to the famous pass, Beckwourth, California, is also named after him. There is also a Jim Beckwourth museum in Plumas County, California.

Gold brought another African American, named Moses Rodgers, to California. Rodgers was born into slavery in Missouri in 1835 and worked in mining on the East Coast. When the California gold rush began in 1848 with the discovery of gold at Sutter's Mill, the man who owned Rodgers sent him there to find out whether the gold strike was rich enough to warrant starting a mine. Historian Leon Ross explains that because California was admitted to the Union in 1850 as a free state that prohibited slavery, that decision gave Rodgers his freedom: "His master sent him out here to find out what was going on about all this stuff they heard about in California. When he came [to California] and found out he was free he decided to stay."[17] Rodgers became a successful mining engineer and in 1878 built a lavish home in Stockton, California. It was later placed on the National Register of Historic Places. A plaque there identifies him as "one of California's leading Black citizens."[18]

## Slaves Built the Capitol

The White House and the buildings and grounds of the Capitol in Washington, D.C., are sacred landmarks and symbols of the United States. Yet they are also African American landmarks

# Slaves and the U.S. Capitol

The work African American slaves did is still visible in many places in the United States. The White House and Capitol in Washington, D.C., are the most historic buildings still standing that slaves built. In 2009, just days before Barack Obama was inaugurated as the nation's first African American president, Jesse Holland, who wrote *Black Men Built the Capitol*, said:

> One of the things that I found was that actual African-American slaves were used in the construction of the U.S. Capitol and the White House. Out of just about the 600 or so people who worked on the Capitol, maybe about 400 were African-American slaves. [The area] where Barack Obama [will take] his oath of office used to be a tent city for these slaves and workers. [What] a lot of people don't know about the National Mall, Capitol, [and] Supreme Court area is that African-American slaves were held in bondage in slave jails on some of these sites.

Jesse Holland. "Author Offers Insights on Slavery, Inauguration." *Video ClipBoard* (blog), *PBS NewsHour*, January 16, 2009. www.pbs.org/newshour/extra/video/blog/2009/01/slaves_built_the_white_house_u.html.

THIS SANDSTONE WAS ORIGINALLY PART OF THE UNITED STATES CAPITOL'S EAST FRONT, CONSTRUCTED IN 1824-1826. IT WAS QUARRIED BY LABORERS, INCLUDING ENSLAVED AFRICAN AMERICANS, AND COMMEMORATES THEIR IMPORTANT ROLE IN BUILDING THE CAPITOL.

Dedicated in 2009, this plaque in the U.S. Capitol commemorates the role of slaves in its construction.

because slaves built them. On June 16, 2010, the slaves responsible for the physical grandeur of those buildings were finally honored. In a ceremony in the halls of Congress, two plaques were dedicated to their long-ago efforts in building the structure that houses Congress. Representative John Lewis, who is also a hero of the civil rights movement, said the honor was fitting and long overdue: "The history of the Capitol, like the history of our nation should be complete. With these plaques . . . we recognize the blood sweat and toil of the enslaved African Americans that helped construct this embodiment of our democracy. . . . We are one step closer to realizing a dream of an all inclusive and more perfect union."[19]

## Chapter Two

# African Americans Resist Slavery

For nearly 250 years, millions of African Americans lived as slaves. Racists sometimes claim that slavery would not have lasted so long if blacks had not willingly accepted the bondage whites imposed on them. Historical evidence, however, shows that Africans resisted their enslavement and fought for their freedom throughout the slavery era event though they knew their resistance would mean death or punishment. For example, on June 23, 1855, when Robert Newsom tried to force a slave named Celia to have sex, she beat him to death with a stick. Celia was hanged on December 21, 1855, for killing him even though she was only trying to stop him from raping her, not letting her owner do what he wanted with her. Thousands of slaves risked punishment by running away—slaves who failed to escape were whipped and branded—and there were at least 250 slave rebellions in which ten or more slaves banded together to fight for their freedom.

Historian Lerone Bennett Jr. writes that slaves also protested their enslavement in many small ways. They refused to work hard for masters they hated, broke farm implements to sabotage their work, and committed other acts that denied whites the full benefit of their labor. Bennett claims that the sum total of slave resistance proves African Americans did not docilely accept an unjust system that denied them their freedom: "[In a variety of ways] they quietly and subtly and deliberately sabotaged [slavery] from within. By resisting, maintaining, enduring and abiding, by holding on and holding fast and holding out, they provided one of the greatest examples in history of the strength of the human spirit in adversity."[20] This resistance sometimes began even as Africans were being transported to their new lives as slaves.

## The Amistad Revolt

On September 18, 1992, a 14-foot-high bronze memorial (4.3m) was dedicated in New Haven, Connecticut, to honor Sengbe Pieh, an African who in 1839 led a revolt aboard the Spanish slave ship *Amistad* (Spanish for "Friendship"). The memorial has three 10-foot images (3m) of Pieh that depict him as a warrior in his native Sierra Leone, a scene from a trial in New Haven for Pieh and fifty-two other blacks charged with mutiny and murder, and Pieh's triumphant return home after the Africans won a legal battle for their freedom.

Fifty-three slaves were aboard the *Amistad* on June 27, 1839, when it sailed from Havana to another city in the Spanish colony of Cuba. On July 2 Pieh, whose slave name was Cinqué, freed himself and other slaves from the chains that imprisoned them. They killed the ship's captain and all the sailors except for two, who agreed to return them to Africa. Instead, the Spaniards betrayed them by sailing north along the coast of the United States. On August 26 the U.S. Navy seized the ship after it had anchored near Long Island, New York, to buy food and water.

When the captured slaves were arrested, northern whites opposed to slavery filed a lawsuit to free them. Participants in the legal battle included former president John Adams, who defended the slaves; Great Britain, which opposed slavery; and Spain, which claimed it owned the slaves and wanted to punish them for trying to escape. After two years of legal arguments, the Supreme Court ruled on March 9, 1841, that the slaves did not belong to Spain and ordered them freed. Thirty-five survivors left for their

The Amistad Memorial in New Haven, Connecticut, commemorates the revolt of African slaves against their Spanish captors aboard the slave ship *Amistad*.

homeland on November 27, 1841, after people who opposed slavery had donated enough money to pay for their passage back to Africa.

The monument honoring Pieh and the revolt is on the former site of the jail where the Africans were held during the trials.

Across from the site is New Haven Green, where the Africans were allowed to exercise daily. The monument is also near Center Church, where local residents first gathered to support the imprisoned Africans. The memorial is one of more than twenty historic sites linked to the *Amistad* in Connecticut. One of them is Riverdale Cemetery in Farmington, where the African Foone is buried; he drowned three months before he was to return home.

The *Amistad* case did not end slavery in the United States, because the high court had only ruled on the legality of the international slave trade. The United States had banned importation of slaves in 1807, even though it still allowed slaves already living within its borders to be bought and sold. However, historian

## A Successful Runaway Slave

Barney L. Ford was born a slave on January 22, 1822, at Stafford Courthouse, Virginia. When he was seventeen years old, Barney—his only name as a slave—escaped to freedom in Chicago via the Underground Railroad. Barney learned to read and began to dream of a successful life. He also married Julia Lyon and took the last name of Ford. The couple moved to Colorado in 1860, and Ford started a barbershop. He was a successful businessperson who eventually owned three restaurants and the Inter-Ocean Hotel, and he funded profitable gold-mining ventures. Ford fought for African American civil rights by leading the fight to make sure Colorado gave blacks the right to vote when it became a state in 1876. Today the Barney Ford House Museum in Breckenridge, Colorado, is dedicated to educating the public about Ford and other people of color in Colorado's history. Ford's biography on a Colorado state website praises him: "He was a leading activist for the rights of African-Americans. . . . Ford was also the first black man to sit on a Grand Jury in Colorado and is responsible for ensuring that the State Constitution allowed 'all males' the right to vote."

Colorado State Capitol Virtual Tour. "Barney Ford." June 30, 2003. www.colorado.gov/dpa/doit/archives/cap/bford.htm.

Howard Jones claims the *Amistad* ruling gave new hope to African American slaves:

> The importance of the *Amistad* case lies in the fact that Cinqué and his fellow captives, in collaboration with white abolitionists, had won their freedom and thereby encouraged others to continue the struggle. [It also showed the need] to change the Constitution and American laws [to comply] with the moral principles underlying the Declaration of Independence [that all men are created equal].[21]

It was one of the few revolts, either on ships or by slaves once they reached the United States, that was successful. African Americans, however, never stopped trying to win their freedom.

## Slave Rebellions

The earliest slave revolt occurred on April 6, 1712, in New York City, which had one of the largest colonial slave populations. About thirty slaves and free blacks set fire to buildings and used guns, clubs, and knives to kill nine men and wound a half-dozen other whites. Whites quickly suppressed the uprising, arresting seventy blacks and executing twenty-one of them by brutal methods such as burning them to death. Their bodies are buried in the African Burial Ground in Manhattan, a cemetery for New York slaves that is a National Historic Landmark and is near the site of the uprising. The severity of their punishment for resisting slavery did not stop other blacks from trying to win their freedom.

One of the panels on the African-American History Monument in Columbia, South Carolina, depicts slave uprisings because South Carolina had two of the most famous slave rebellions—the Stono Rebellion and one led by Denmark Vesey, a free black. On U.S. Highway 17 near Rantowles, South Carolina, a plaque on the west bank of Wallace Creek commemorates the Stono Rebellion. The plaque reads:

> The Stono Rebellion, the largest slave insurrection in British North America, began nearby on September 6, 1739. About twenty Africans raided a store on Wallace Creek, a branch of the Stono River. Taking guns and other weapons, they

killed two shopkeepers. The rebels marched south toward promised freedom in Spanish Florida, waving flags, beating drums, and shouting "Liberty."[22]

A slave named Jemmy led the Stono Rebellion, the largest slave uprising in colonial times. Eventually, about sixty slaves joined Jemmy in an attempt to escape to Florida, which at the time was known as a refuge for escaped slaves. The slaves killed an estimated twenty-five whites before being defeated by local militia. Slaves who were not killed in the fighting or executed were sold in the West Indies.

A roadside marker near Charleston, South Carolina, marks the site of the 1739 Stono Rebellion, the largest slave insurrection in the history of British North America.

Another slave uprising occurred after a slave named Vesey won six hundred dollars in a lottery in 1799, enough money to buy his freedom but not that of his wife and children. Their continued enslavement angered Vesey so much that he persuaded other South Carolina blacks to revolt against whites. On July 14, 1822, thousands of free blacks and slaves were set to attack whites and seize the city of Charleston. But whites learned of the plan and arrested Vesey and thirty-five other blacks before they could begin the revolt. All of them were hanged for daring to attack whites to win their freedom.

Vesey was considered a criminal in 1822 but today is hailed as an early fighter for black civil rights. In 1976 Vesey's home in Charleston was declared a National Historic Landmark. And in February 2010 a monument to his heroic stand against

## George Boxley Cabin

The George Boxley Cabin in Adams Township, Indiana, was placed on the National Register of Historic Places in 2000. Boxley built the cabin in 1828 when he became the first white settler in the area, and he allowed the cabin to be used as a safe house for the Underground Railroad. However, it has another connection to black history through Boxley, who in 1815 tried to start a slave rebellion in Spotsylvania, Virginia. Boxley was born in Virginia in 1780 and became a storekeeper and businessperson. He owned slaves when he was younger, but he eventually decided slavery was wrong and freed them. He began helping slaves escape and educating them at his store by reading antislavery articles that demonstrated many whites believed slavery should be abolished. He also tried to get slaves in Orange, Spotsylvania, and Louisa Counties to join him in taking control of the cities of Fredericksburg and Richmond. The slave revolt was supposed to begin at his home on March 6, 1815, but a slave named Lucy who knew about it told her master about the planned uprising. Whites arrested Boxley and some of the blacks before they could start the slave revolt. Boxley escaped from jail in May when his wife, Hannah, smuggled a saw into his jail cell in the hem of her skirt. Boxley fled the area and was never caught.

The South Carolina home of Denmark Vesey, a freed slave who planned an 1822 slave insurrection, is now a National Historic Landmark.

slavery was erected in Charleston's Hampton Park. The monument features a bronze statue of Vesey and two other leaders of the planned uprising—Peter Poyas and Jack "Gullah Jack" Purcell—that sits atop a 5-foot granite pedestal (1.5m). Some white Charleston residents had opposed a monument for Vesey because they felt he had been wrong to want to use violence to free other slaves. Mayor Joe Riley, however, claimed it was important to honor him. Riley said Vesey is part of the "substantially untold story of African-American history and life in this community and this country, and their role in building America. We tell these untold stories so the truth will set us free."[23]

Feelings were also mixed in 1991 when the Virginia Department of Historic Resources put up an historical marker for Nat Turner's Insurrection, the bloodiest slave revolt in U.S. history. On August 21, 1831, Nathaniel "Nat" Turner and six other slaves killed their master, Joseph Travis, and the rest of his family. They traveled to nearby plantations to kill whites, seize weapons, and recruit other slaves, seventy of whom joined Turner. Although the slaves killed sixty white men, women, and children, Turner spared poor whites who did not own slaves. Local militias quelled the uprising in two days, but Turner was not captured until October 30. Turner was convicted of rebelling against whites and was hanged on November 11 in Jerusalem (now Courtland), Virginia. Turner was also beheaded and his body chopped into pieces. Officials executed another fifty-six blacks for their involvement. White citizens were so angry and fearful of slave revolts that they also murdered nearly two hundred more slaves, even though many of them had not participated in the rebellion and were only suspected of having been involved in the incident.

Mass uprisings failed to earn blacks their freedom. However, many African Americans did escape slavery by fleeing to areas of the country where it was illegal.

## Escaping Slavery

Slavery continued in the South until the end of the Civil War, but northern states began making it illegal not long after the American Revolution began. On July 2, 1777, Vermont became the first state to outlaw slavery, and by 1804 every state north of Delaware had prohibited it. Because slavery was illegal in northern states, slaves were freed if they could travel there.

Henry "Box" Brown was born a slave in Virginia in 1815, and by 1830 he had been taken to Richmond by his master to work in a tobacco factory. While working in Richmond Brown married a woman named Nancy, and they had children together. In 1848 when his wife and three children were sold to a slave trader and taken away, Brown decided to seek his freedom. With the help of several whites, Brown had himself sent in a box to James Miller McKim, a Philadelphia man who opposed slavery. His trip to freedom in Pennsylvania began on March 23, 1849, and lasted twenty-seven hours. The box was small—3 feet (91cm) long, 2.5 feet (76cm) deep, and 2 feet (61cm) wide—and Brown suffered physically when the box was turned around and upside down during the trip. But freedom was worth the discomfort to Brown. In honor of his ingenious method of escape, a metal reproduction of the box and a plaque explaining how Brown used it to gain his freedom is prominently displayed today on Canal Walk in downtown Richmond.

Barney L. Ford was born a slave on January 22, 1822, in Virginia. When Ford was seventeen, he escaped to Chicago and freedom. Ford was one of thousands of blacks who were freed by the Underground Railroad, the name for a vast network of blacks and whites in both the North and South who helped slaves escape to states where slavery was illegal. The system provided slaves with secret travel routes, safe houses where they stayed on their journey, and help in starting new lives as free men and women.

The home of the Reverend John Rankin in Ripley, Ohio, is one of sixty Underground Railroad sites designated National Historic Landmarks.

It is believed the Underground Railroad helped as many as one hundred thousand African Americans escape slavery.

The Underground Railroad operated in twenty-one states and the District of Columbia. The National Park Service lists sixty Underground Railroad sites as historic landmarks, including the Barney L. Ford Building in Denver, where Ford eventually moved and became a successful businessman; Milton House in Milton, Wisconsin; and the St. James AME Zion Church in Ithaca, New York. Cities and states have also designated many other Underground Railroad sites as historic landmarks.

People began calling this system the Underground Railroad around 1840, even though railroads were not a major part of its transportation system. Because of its name, people who helped slaves escape became known by the railroad term *conductor*. One of the most famous conductors was Frederick Douglass, a freed slave who became one of the most powerful leaders in the movement to abolish slavery.

## Abolishing Slavery

Douglass was born in February 1818 in Talbot County, Maryland. Unlike most slaves, Douglass learned to read and write, and his ability to read newspapers and books made him determined to become free. Douglass had tried to escape twice before he succeeded on September 3, 1838, when he used identity papers from a free black to board a train and travel to New York. Douglass wrote several books, including an autobiography that included his dramatic description of slave life. He also spoke against slavery in the United States and Europe, published the *North Star* and other abolitionist newspapers, and aided the Underground Railroad.

Douglass was an eloquent speaker who was never more powerful than when he described the hardships of slave life. On September 12, 1846, in Sheffield, England, he told an audience:

> The slave has no rights; he is a being with all the capacities of a man in the condition of the brute. [The] slave-holder decides what he shall eat or drink, when and to whom he shall speak, when he shall work, and how long he shall work; when he shall marry, and how long the marriage shall be binding, and what shall be the cause of its dissolution— what is right and wrong, virtue or vice.[24]

Abolitionist and former slave Frederick C. Douglass's Cedar Hill House in Washington, D.C., is now a National Historic Site.

His vivid portrayal of slavery and dramatic arguments against it helped persuade many people to join the fight to abolish slavery. Douglass, the nineteenth century's most famous African American, went on to be an adviser to Abraham Lincoln and was named ambassador to the Dominican Republic. There are many historic sites that honor his accomplishments, including Cedar Hill, the Washington, D.C., home he lived in from 1877 until his death in 1895. The home is a National Historic Site open to the public.

Another escaped slave who became a well-known historical figure was Sojourner Truth, who was born in Swartekill, New York, in 1797. In 1826 when she was no longer able to tolerate living with a cruel master, she escaped bondage with her infant daughter just a year before New York made slavery illegal. Truth, however, had been forced to leave her three other children behind when she left.

# Dred Scott

Most African American historical sites honor positive historical events or black achievements, but some are reminders of slavery. Several of the latter are associated with Dred Scott, a runaway slave involved in a historic court case that upheld slavery. In 1857 Scott filed a lawsuit claiming he, his wife, and two daughters should be freed because they had previously lived with his owner in areas that prohibited slavery, including Minnesota. In a major blow to black rights, the U.S. Supreme Court ruled on March 6, 1857, that people of African descent, whether slave or free, were not citizens of the United States. The high court said because he was not a citizen, Scott could not legally file a lawsuit to seek his freedom. But on May 26 the Scotts were freed anyway. Scott's owner had died and willed them to a family member who opposed slavery and gave them their freedom. The *Dred Scott* decision sharpened the bitter feelings between northern and south-

ern states and is considered one of the factors in igniting the Civil War. The Old Court House in St. Louis is a National Historic Landmark for many reasons, including that it was where Scott filed his lawsuit. And Fort Snelling State Park in Minneapolis is where Scott lived as a slave from 1836 to 1840, when his owner, John Emerson, was stationed at the U.S. Army post.

The Old Court House in Saint Louis, Missouri, a National Historic Landmark, is best known as the site where Dred Scott filed his historic lawsuit.

After New York abolished slavery, she discovered her five-year-old son, Peter, had been illegally sold to someone in Alabama. With the help of a white family that aided her after her escape, Truth filed a lawsuit and got her son back. Truth traveled extensively in the next few decades to speak against slavery. She also adopted the cause of women's rights—women then could not vote or own property in most states—and on May 29, 1851, gave her famous "Ain't I a Woman" speech at the Women's Convention in Akron, Ohio.

Many monuments and historic sites honor the work Truth did for African Americans and women. They include a statue and her gravesite in Battle Creek, Michigan, where she lived after the Civil War. And on April 28, 2009, Truth became the first African American woman to have a memorial bust placed in the U.S. Capitol. Michelle Obama attended the ceremony to unveil the statue. Obama said: "I hope that Sojourner Truth would be proud to see me, a descendant of slaves, serving as the First Lady of the United States of America. [The] power of this bust will not just be in the metal that delineates Sojourner Truth's face; it will also be in the message [of freedom] that defines her legacy."[25]

## "But with Blood"

Many whites helped African Americans escape slavery and worked to abolish slavery. One of them, John Brown, used violence. On October 16, 1859, Brown led a misguided and failed attempt to steal weapons from the U.S. Arsenal at Harpers Ferry, Virginia. Brown wanted to arm blacks for a revolt to end slavery, but U.S. Marines led by Brevet Colonel Robert E. Lee overpowered Brown's small band of whites and blacks. Brown was found guilty of treason and hanged on December 2 in Charles Town, Virginia (later Charleston, West Virginia). Before his death, Brown gave a note to a jail attendant that read: "I John Brown am now quite certain that the crimes of this guilty land [slavery] will never be purged away but with blood."[26] Brown's prophecy was correct. The Civil War began sixteen months later, with Lee fighting as the top general for the Confederate States of America.

Several historic sites honor Brown, including the John Brown Museum in Osawatomie, Kansas, and the John Brown Farm State Historic Site in Lake Placid, New York, where Brown and several of his followers are buried.

## Chapter Three

# The Civil War

The Lincoln Memorial in Washington, D.C., is a dramatic landmark honoring the person many historians believe was the nation's greatest president. Built in the style of a Greek temple, the monument on the National Mall was dedicated on May 30, 1922. It is 99 feet (30m) tall with sides measuring 189.7 feet (57.8m) and 118.5 feet (36m) and is surrounded by 36 columns that are 44 feet (13m) tall. Dominating the interior of the massive marble monument is a giant statue of a seated Lincoln 19 feet (5.8m) tall, made of 159 tons (144.2t) of Georgia white marble. A plaque on the statue reads, "In this temple, as in the hearts of the people for whom he saved the Union, the memory of Abraham Lincoln is enshrined forever."[27]

Lincoln was one of the most eloquent speakers ever elected president. Two of his most famous speeches—his second inaugural address in 1865 and the Gettysburg Address—are carved into the walls of chambers adjoining the main one containing his statue. Lincoln delivered his speech at Gettysburg, Pennsylvania, on November 19, 1863, to dedicate a cemetery for tens of thousands of soldiers who died in July 1863 during the second battle of Gettysburg. His address, perhaps the greatest ever given by a president, ended with this promise: "From these honored dead we take increased devotion to that cause for which they here, gave the last full measure of devotion—that we here highly resolve these dead shall not have died in vain; that the nation, shall have a new birth of freedom, and that government of the people by the people for the people, shall not perish from the earth."[28]

These two quotations from the Lincoln Memorial are significant because they reflect how his goals in fighting the war changed from 1861 to 1865. Lincoln's only desire at first was to preserve the Union. But as the war continued, Lincoln realized that the most important reason underlying the conflict was to end slavery, a goal historians claim he referred to with the phrase "new birth of freedom" in his Gettysburg Address.

Lincoln managed to perform both historic tasks. However, his election in 1860 was also what catapulted the nation into civil war.

## How the War Started

Slavery had been legal in every state for nearly a century after the first African Americans arrived in Virginia in 1619. However, by 1804 slavery had become a controversial, divisive issue between

The Lincoln Memorial in Washington, D.C., was dedicated in 1922 and honors Abraham Lincoln, whom the majority of historians believe to be the greatest U.S. president.

North and South because northern states had all outlawed it. In the next six decades, escaped slave Frederick Douglass and other abolitionists convinced more and more people that slavery should be abolished entirely. Lincoln himself became a national leader of this cause after his speech on June 16, 1858, in Springfield, Illinois, in which he declared, "A house divided against itself cannot stand. I believe this government cannot endure permanently half slave and half free."[29] Today the Old State Capitol building in which Lincoln delivered that speech is a state historic site.

This growing antislavery sentiment helped Lincoln win election on November 6, 1860. Lincoln's victory made southern states fearful he would outlaw slavery, a source of cheap labor southerners believed they needed because their economies were based on agriculture. Within a few months after Lincoln's election, eleven

Lincoln gave his famous "A House Divided Against Itself Cannot Stand" speech in 1858 at the Old State Capitol in Springfield, Illinois.

southern states had seceded from the Union and formed the Confederate States of America. In his inaugural speech on March 4, 1861, Lincoln tried to make peace with the South by promising not to force individual states to outlaw slavery. However, he also warned southern states that they did not have the right to secede and that he would do everything he could to make them remain part of the United States. A little more than a month later, the Civil War began on April 12, 1861, when Confederate forces attacked Fort Sumter in South Carolina. The fort is now a national monument.

The Civil War would eventually end slavery, but when the war began, neither Lincoln nor other U.S. officials knew what to do with the thousands of slaves who gained their freedom during the war.

## Contraband or Free People?

On May 23, 1861, shortly after the war began, Shepard Mallory, Frank Baker, and James Townsend escaped from soldiers forcing them to build defenses for the Confederate army and went to nearby Fort Monroe in Hampton, Virginia, to seek their freedom. Fort Monroe, now a national monument, was the largest stone fort ever built in the United States; U.S. soldiers still controlled the imposing fortress even though it was in Confederate territory. The arrival of the escaped slaves provided the first test the United States faced during the war over their status.

When Confederate major John B. Cary asked the army to return the slaves, Brigadier General Benjamin Butler was not sure what to do. Runaway slaves had usually been returned to their owners in the past if the owners demanded it, but freeing slaves had not yet become a U.S. goal in the war. Butler decided that because the Confederates believed the men were property, he would consider them contraband of war, a military term for property soldiers seize from the enemy. Although Butler did not have the power to free the slaves, he denied Cary's request to return them and instead hired them as army laborers.

The issue over the status of escaped slaves soon grew more intense because thousands of slaves fled to Union-held territory seeking their freedom. Most officers followed Butler's example in handling them, but some returned slaves to their owners. On

## Aunt Betty Calls Lincoln a Fool

Elizabeth Proctor Thomas and her husband, James, owned a small farm near Washington, D.C. When the Civil War began, the government confiscated it to build Fort Wagner to protect the nation's capital against invasion by the Confederate army. Thomas told a reporter how Abraham Lincoln himself apologized to her, saying, "It is hard, but you shall reap a great reward."[1] The family later got the land back. Thomas wound up cooking for the soldiers and had another encounter with Lincoln that was even more dramatic. On July 9, 1864, Lincoln visited Fort Wagner to watch Union troops battle Confederate soldiers. When Thomas saw Lincoln watching from a parapet of the fort, she is said to have shouted, "Get down you fool."[2] It was sound advice—a surgeon standing near Lincoln was wounded, forcing Lincoln finally to seek cover. Historical markers that are part of the Defense of Washington series explain the sacrifice made by the woman known as "Aunt Betty."

1. Quoted in Historical Marker Database. "Aunt Betty's Story." www.hmdb.org/marker.asp?marker=17132.
2. Quoted in Historical Marker Database. "'Get Down You Fool.'" www.hmdb.org/Marker.asp?Marker=17133.

August 6, 1861, Congress passed the Confiscation Act of 1861 to set a consistent policy on escaped slaves. The act did not state the slaves were free but claimed their former owners no longer had any legal right to them.

The result of the act was that most escaping slaves became workers for the army or government agencies. By 1863 an estimated ten thousand blacks from Virginia and Maryland were living and working in Washington, D.C., and that number quadrupled by the end of the war. Most of them labored to build Fort Stevens and other defensive positions around the nation's capital designed to repel enemy attacks. Black laborers did such a good job that civil engineer Edward Frost praised them in a letter to General William Denison Whipple. Frost wrote that "the contraband were important to the construction and maintenance of the defense of Washington. Without the contrabands' numbers and labor, the defenses would not have been as successful as they were."[30] The Defense of Washington series of historic markers honor their work today by pointing out where defensive positions like Fort Stevens once stood and explaining how African Americans built them.

As the army freed more slaves by winning control of Confederate territory, the question of what would happen to them after the war ended became a pressing issue. One notable person demanding an answer about their future was Frederick Douglass.

Fort Monroe in Hampton, Virginia, the largest stone fort built in the United States, is now a National Historic Monument partly due to its role in determining the status of captured and escaped slaves during the Civil War.

## "What Shall Be Their Status?"

After Douglass escaped from slavery in 1838, he lived in Rochester, New York, for twenty-five years. There are many historic sites in Rochester linked to Douglass, including Mount Hope Cemetery, where Douglass is buried; a home he once owned; and his statue in Frederick Douglass Memorial Park. In the January 1862 issue of *Douglass' Monthly*, one of several abolitionist publications he wrote and edited, Douglass expressed his concern about the fate of freed slaves: "What shall be their status in the new condition of things? Shall they exchange the relation of slavery to individuals, only to become the slaves of the community at large, having no rights which anybody is required to respect [or] shall they have secured to them equal rights before the law."[31]

Douglass, of course, believed slaves should be freed and given equal rights with whites. Many whites, including Lincoln, were not sure whether blacks were worthy of rights such as voting in elections, but as the war continued Lincoln began to realize that blacks, at the very least, should no longer have to live in bondage, and he decided the time had come to free them. As Lincoln put it, "The moment came when I felt that slavery must die that the nation might live."[32] On January 1, 1863, Lincoln used his war powers as president to issue an executive order known as the Emancipation Proclamation to free slaves in southern states still fighting in the war. The full impact of his order was not realized until the end of the conflict two years later. However, the date of his proclamation is considered the date in which, for all practical purposes, slavery in the United States ended.

Lincoln's proclamation also allowed African Americans to fight in the war. Freed slaves and free blacks had been begging for the right to enlist in the U.S. Army ever since the war began. The United States had allowed blacks to serve in menial positions on U.S. naval ships for many years, but it would not let them join the army. Douglass also argued blacks should be able to fight in the war because he believed it would show that they were worthy of becoming U.S. citizens. Douglass wrote: "Once let the black man get upon his person the brass letter, U.S., let him get an eagle on his button, and a musket on his shoulder and bullets in his pocket, there is no power on earth that can deny that he has earned the right to citizenship."[33]

# Confederate Landmarks

There are many historic sites and landmarks in the South linked to the Civil War. On May 29, 1890, the Lee Monument Association dedicated a bronze statue in Richmond, Virginia, of General Robert E. Lee. The 21-foot-high figure (6.4m) of Lee mounted on a horse sits atop a 40-foot-high granite pedestal (12.2m). Many other sites honor the popular Confederate general, including Arlington House, Lee's former home in Arlington, Virginia, which is a National Historic Site dedicated to him. Some southern historic sites mention slavery. Although slaves were forced to work as laborers for the Confederate army, a site in York County, South Carolina, praises them for willingly aiding the war effort. In 1895 Samuel E. White and members of the Jefferson Davis Memorial Association dedicated a stone marker to honor slaves they claimed faithfully supported the war to uphold principles of the Confederacy, which included slavery. Historian Kirk Savage ridicules that idea and claims, "It was a monument generated from a former slaveholder's perspective, designed not to celebrate slavery's demise but to muse nostalgically over its passing."

Kirk Savage. *Standing Soldiers, Kneeling Slaves: Race, War, and Monument in Nineteenth-Century America*. Princeton, NJ: Princeton University Press, 1997, p. 157.

The West Point Monument in Norfolk, Virginia, is one of few in the South dedicated to black Civil War veterans.

Tens of thousands of blacks immediately enlisted in the army. By the end of the conflict, 179,000 blacks had served in the army, 19,000 had served in the navy, and 40,000 had been killed. They worked as carpenters, cooks, guards, laborers, and spies and also fought in combat units. Today hundreds of memorials and historic landmarks honor the heroic service of African Americans to a nation that had allowed them to be enslaved for generations. One of the most dramatic memorials honors the most-celebrated black military units of the war—the Fifty-Fourth Massachusetts Regiment.

## Blacks Fight for Freedom

On May 31, 1897, a memorial for Colonel Robert Gould Shaw and the Fifty-Fourth Massachusetts Regiment was dedicated in Boston. The giant sculpture by Augustus Saint-Gaudens—it is 11 feet (3.4m) tall and 14 feet (4.3m) wide—depicts Shaw and

The Shaw memorial in New Hampshire commemorates the African American soldiers of the Fifty-Fourth Massachussetts Regiment, which distinguished itself during the Civil War.

sixteen members of one of the first black units in the Civil War. Mounted on a horse, Shaw follows a drummer boy, while soldiers march behind him. Historian Kirk Savage explains that for many decades after the war, most monuments honoring Union soldiers did not credit or depict African Americans because of racist attitudes toward blacks. But Savage wrote that Saint-Gaudens's work honored the black soldiers Shaw led into battle, as well as their white officer: "[Both officer and troops] are absorbed in a common mission, and that mission is represented most profoundly by the men on the ground in their compelling martial presence. [They] move forward out of the relief and into our space, acquiring a concreteness and individuality that African Americans never before had in public sculpture."[34]

The all-black regiment, which included many freed slaves, became famous on July 18, 1863, in the battle to take Fort Wagner, an island fortress in Charleston, South Carolina. Union forces failed to capture the fort, but the Fifty-Fourth Regiment fought heroically, and Sergeant William Harvey Carney became the first African American to win the Medal of Honor for his actions that day. Shaw died in the fierce fighting along with fifty-three of his men. Before that battle, many whites had believed blacks lacked the courage or intelligence to function well in combat. But the bravery the Fifty-Fourth Regiment displayed convinced the army blacks could help win the war, and the army created more African American units.

The Medal of Honor, the nation's highest award for bravery, was first given during the Civil War. Twenty-five blacks received it, including Powhatan Beaty, who was born a slave in Richmond, Virginia, in 1837. On September 29, 1864, Beaty was a first sergeant in the Fifth U.S. Colored Infantry during the Battle of Chaffin's Farm in Virginia. When officers in his company were killed, Beaty took command of the unit and was cited for gallantry in leading them on a charge that drove Confederate soldiers from their fortified position. Beaty's heroism is cited in one of fifty-eight historical markers at National Battlefield Park in Richmond, Virginia.

Hundreds of historic sites, monuments, and markers honor individual African American soldiers and military units. One that honors all of them is the African American Civil War Memorial

The African American Civil War Memorial in Washington, D.C., is inscribed with the names of the black soldiers, sailors, and women who fought in the war.

in Washington, D.C. A 9-foot-tall bronze sculpture (2.7m) titled *Spirit of Freedom* dominates the memorial, which includes curved panels with the names of the black soldiers and sailors who fought in the war. The memorial is near the African American Civil War Museum, which tells the story of black soldiers through photographs, printed material, and replicas of weapons and uniforms.

The *Spirit of Freedom* sculpture included a black woman as well as several soldiers. No women then could join the army, but many served as cooks, nurses, and spies. One woman—Harriet Tubman—even led a military mission into enemy territory during the war that freed more than 750 slaves.

## Harriet Tubman

Tubman was born a slave in 1820 in Dorchester County, Maryland, but in 1849 escaped to Pennsylvania with the help of the Underground Railroad. She began working with the Underground Railroad and in thirteen trips south guided more than seventy slaves to freedom, including members of her own family. Tubman was soon nicknamed "Moses" after the biblical figure who led Hebrews out of slavery in Egypt. Her most daring exploit came when she led a Union army force that included 150 soldiers of the black Second South Carolina Regiment on a raid into South Carolina. Army officers even asked the former slave to help plan the raid because she knew the area and had sources there for information on Confederate troop movements.

On June 1, 1863, Tubman guided three Union gunboats down the Combahee River on a mission to disrupt Confederate supply lines by destroying railroad tracks and bridges. On the return trip, hundreds of slaves gathered along the river, and the boats picked them up and carried them to freedom. To encourage blacks to escape, Tubman sang, "Of all the whole creation in the East or in the West, the glorious Yankee nation is the greatest and the best. Come

## West Point Monument to Black Soldiers

The West Point monument in Elmwood Cemetery in Norfolk, Virginia, is one of the few in the South to honor African American Civil War veterans. James E. Fuller, a former slave and Civil War veteran who was the first black elected to the city council, initiated the tribute to black soldiers. The monument features a statue of First Sergeant William Harvey Carney, a Norfolk native and Medal of Honor winner who fought with the famed Fifty-Fourth Massachusetts Regiment. The statue, which was dedicated in 1920, shows Carney standing at ease and holding a rifle atop a tall stone column. Carney is most famous for his role in the attack on Fort Wagner on July 18, 1863. A historical marker explains that Carney, despite being wounded, kept the regiment's U.S. flag from being captured when soldiers carrying it were shot. The marker quotes Carney as saying, "When they saw me bringing in the colors, they cheered me, and I was able to tell them that the old flag never touched the ground." He won the Medal of Honor for that act of bravery.

Quoted in Historical Marker Database. "West Point Monument Norfolk's Civil War African American Heritage." www.hmdb.org/marker.asp?marker=29415.

along! Come along! Don't be alarmed, Uncle Sam is right enough to give you all a farm!"—and at the end of every verse slaves who climbed aboard the boats would shout, "Glory."[35]

A story in a Boston newspaper about the raid described a "speech from the black woman, who led the raid and under whose inspiration it was originated and conducted. For sound sense and real native eloquence, her address would do honor to any man, and it created a great sensation."[36] The newspaper did not name Tubman, but in 2006 the South Carolina State Legislature honored her by naming a U.S. Highway bridge over the Combahee River after her. The bridge, one of many historic sites honoring Tubman, is just south of where historians believe the raid took place.

Until the war ended, Tubman continued to help the Union army as a spy and nurse. Tubman was at the battle for Fort Wagner and even served Colonel Shaw his last meal. This is her vivid account of the Union's attempt to take the Confederate fort: "And then we saw the lightning, and that was the guns; and then we heard the thunder, and that was the big guns; and then we heard the rain falling, and that was the drops of blood falling; and when we came to get the crops, it was dead men that we reaped."[37]

## The Freedmen's Memorial

More than 360,000 Union troops sacrificed their lives to win the Civil War and end slavery. Another casualty of the conflict was Lincoln, who died April 15, 1865, after being shot by John Wilkes Booth, a southerner who was angry the South had lost. Although the Lincoln Memorial is the best-known landmark honoring the slain president, the first was the Freedmen's Memorial in Lincoln Square in Washington, D.C. The memorial features a bronze statue of Lincoln. His left hand is extended over a kneeling slave whose shackles have been broken, and his right hand touches a copy of the Emancipation Proclamation. Written in large letters on the pedestal of the statue is the word EMANCIPATION.

The statue was paid for entirely by freed slaves. The fund-raising effort started when Charlotte Scott of Virginia donated the first five dollars she earned in freedom to begin a memorial to Lincoln. Savage explains that the monument is important because blacks financed it: "The monument asserted their right as citizens to enter the public sphere and the commemorative landscape."[38]

## Chapter Four

# Education for Blacks

The Wye House in Talbot County, Maryland, is a large home built in 1781 that was once the center of a slave plantation encompassing 42,000 acres (16,997ha). It is on the U.S. National Register of Historic Places and is still owned by descendants of Edward Lloyd, who first settled in the area when he moved there in the 1650s from Wales. Descendants of Wye Plantation slaves live in nearby Unionville and Coppertown. Frederick Douglass was born a slave on the plantation sometime in 1818. Douglass was never sure of his birth date because no records were kept of slaves; he later decided to celebrate it on February 14.

After escaping from slavery, Douglass wrote several books in which he vividly described the harsh lives Wye Plantation slaves led. Like most slave children, Douglass was separated from his mother at birth and rarely saw her. Also like almost all slaves, he was not allowed to learn to read or write because southern states prohibited educating slaves. When Douglass was nine, he was sent to Baltimore to work as a slave for Hugh and Sophie Auld. Douglass was so uneducated he could not name the days of the week or months of the year. Sophie treated him with more kindness than any white person ever had. When Douglass was twelve, Sophie began teaching him how to read after he asked her; his desire came from hearing Auld read the Bible out loud

The Wye House in Easton, Maryland, is on the U.S. National Register of Historic Places because Frederick Douglass was born on the owners' plantation sometime in 1818.

daily. Douglass memorized the letters of the alphabet and was soon spelling small words.

Hugh became angry when he learned Sophie was teaching Douglass to read. In a tirade that Douglass overheard, Hugh told his wife she had to stop because educating Douglass would ruin him as a slave. Instead of dulling the young boy's desire to learn, the harsh words made Douglass realize education was the key to helping him escape slavery. He wrote: "His discourse was the first decidedly anti-slavery lecture to which it had been my lot to listen. 'Very well,' thought I. 'Knowledge unfits a child to be a slave.' I instinctively assented to the proposition, and from that moment I understood the direct pathway from slavery to freedom."[39]

Douglass secretly continued his education. The knowledge he acquired about life outside slave plantations made him even more determined to escape. On September 8, 1838, those skills helped Douglass escape when he used the identity papers of a free black to travel to New York, where slavery was illegal. Douglass was not the only slave who managed to get an education even though it was illegal to teach them during most of the slavery era.

## Education During Slavery

South Carolina passed the first law banning education for slaves in 1740 after the Stono Rebellion, and many more states prohibited it after Nat Turner's Rebellion in 1831 in Virginia. Southern states made educating slaves illegal because they believed being

## Thomas Jefferson's Slave Children

—————————— ■ ——————————

Thomas Jefferson was the third president of the United States and author of the Declaration of Independence in 1776, the historic document that stated why the colonies were fighting Great Britain for freedom in the American Revolution. Many historic monuments honor Jefferson, but the Jefferson Memorial in Washington, D.C., is the most significant. The massive yet elegant marble monument on the Potomac River was dedicated on April 13, 1943, the two hundredth anniversary of his birth. It includes a statue of Jefferson 19 feet (5.8m) tall, and its interior walls are engraved with some of his writings. One of the engraved passages is from the Declaration of Independence and includes its most famous line—"that all men are created equal."[1] Despite writing that, Jefferson owned slaves and even had children with one of them, Sally Hemings. Madison Hemings, who is believed to have been Jefferson's son, once said, "I learned to read by inducing [persuading] the white children to teach me the letters."[2] Jefferson could have stopped Madison from doing that. However, like many southerners with slave children, he allowed his son to become educated. He also allowed some valued workers to learn to read and write. When Jefferson died, his will freed Madison Hemings.

1. Quoted in Library of Congress. "Creating the Declaration of Independence." http://myloc.gov /Exhibitions/CreatingtheUS/interactives/declaration/HTML/equal/index.html.
2. Quoted in Monticello Classroom. "Slave Life at Monticello." http://classroom.monticello.org/kids /resources/profile/259/Elementary/Slave-Life-at-Monticello.

able to read and write were skills slaves could use to escape or to communicate with other slaves to plan revolts. Southerners strictly and harshly enforced those laws.

Henry Bibb was born a slave in Shelby County, Kentucky, on May 10, 1815, but in 1850 he escaped to Canada with his wife, Mary. A historical marker in Windsor, Ontario, explains that the freed couple helped many Canadian blacks get an education: "Facing discrimination in the public school system, they established their own schools to improve the education of black children and adults."[40] Henry knew how difficult it was for southern blacks to become educated. In his autobiography, he said that

Slaves Henry Bibb and his wife, Mary, and daughter, Frances, escaped to Canada, where the couple established schools to educate black children and adults.

" *My heart is almost broken.*"

slave patrols—groups of white vigilantes who monitored the activities of blacks—used force to stop attempts to educate slaves:

> Slaves were not allowed books, pen, ink, nor paper, to improve their minds. There was a Miss Davies, a poor white girl, who offered to teach a Sabbath [Sunday] School for the slaves. Books were supplied and she started the school; but the news got to our owners that she was teaching us to read. This caused quite an excitement in the neighborhood. Patrols were appointed to go and break it up the next Sabbath.[41]

Slaves who learned to read often taught other slaves. When the Aulds sent Douglass to work for a planter, he held classes for about forty slaves. When the lessons were discovered, whites armed with clubs and stones broke up the meeting to end the classes. In the 1930s a former Georgia slave interviewed by the Federal Writers' Project explained that her uncle had been severely punished for stealing a book so he could learn to read and write. She said his owner cut off one of her uncle's fingers to warn other blacks not to try to become educated.

Most southern states banned education even for free blacks, but Maryland was an exception. Baltimore had one of the South's largest populations of free blacks—in 1850 the twenty-five thousand free blacks living there made up 15 percent of the city's population. William Watkins was born free in Baltimore in 1803 and in the 1830s operated Watkins' Academy for Negro Youths. The school annually provided a free education for about fifty African American youths. One of his students was Frances Ellen Watkins Harper, a niece whom Watkins and his wife raised after her parents died. Harper became a noted writer of poetry, novels, and essays and earned the nickname the "Bronze Muse." A historical marker in Baltimore honors the accomplishments of one of the nineteenth century's most celebrated African American writers.

Northern blacks could go to school, but there were no free public school systems, and most African Americans could not afford private schools. As a result of that and southern laws against educating blacks, it is estimated that by 1860 only about 5 percent of African Americans nationally were literate. But once the Civil War began, many more blacks began to have the chance to learn that had long been denied them.

## Teaching Freed Slaves

Even before the South surrendered on April 9, 1865, the United States was helping 4 million African Americans freed from slavery learn how to live in freedom. On March 3, 1865, Congress created the Bureau of Refugees, Freedmen and Abandoned Lands, which became known as the Freedmen's Bureau. One of its most important duties was to educate blacks. During Reconstruction, the period that lasted from the end of the war until 1877, the bureau established more than one thousand schools in the South. In addition, religious groups and southern blacks operated two thousand more schools for freed slaves. Georgia is an example of how quickly black education grew. A year after the war ended, at least eight thousand freed slaves were attending school, and eight years later nearly twenty thousand black students were being educated.

## John Chavis

It was not always illegal to teach slaves in southern states. Chavis Park in Raleigh, North Carolina, was named after John Chavis, a free black who was a respected early nineteenth-century Presbyterian minister and educator. The park is near the site of the school where Chavis taught both black and white students. A historical marker that mentions the park reads, "Early nineteenth century free Negro teacher of both races in North Carolina. Memorial park." The marker, dedicated in 1938, was the first in the state to honor an African American. Chavis was born free in Virginia in 1762 and fought in the American Revolution as a teenager. He received a classical education, and his school's curriculum included Greek and Latin. Chavis worked as a respected and successful educator until the Nat Turner Rebellion in 1831. In retaliation for that slave uprising, North Carolina passed laws restricting black rights that included a ban on educating blacks. Chavis died five years later on June 15, 1838. The site of his grave is not known, but Chavis is remembered in North Carolina history.

Quoted in North Carolina Highway Historical Marker Program. "John Chavis." www.ncmarkers.com/Markers.aspx?ct=ddl&sp=search&k=Markers&sv=H-13%20-%20JOHN%20CHAVIS.

The Penn School on Saint Helena Island, South Carolina, was established by the U.S. government in 1862. The plaque commemorates it as the first school for freed slaves in the South.

However, the process of educating freed slaves had begun even earlier. In 1862 the U.S. government established Penn School on Saint Helena Island in Beaufort County, South Carolina, after Union troops won control of it from the Confederacy. Charlotte Forten, a free black from Philadelphia who had taught in northern schools, was one of its first teachers. Forten once wrote that young children, adults, and even older men and women flocked to classes even though many had to work hard most of the day at various jobs: "I never before saw children so eager to learn [and many] of the grown people are desirous of learning to read. It is wonderful how a people who have been so long crushed to the earth can have so great a desire for knowledge, and such a capacity for attaining it."[42]

Forten quit after two years because she became ill. She moved to Washington, D.C., where she worked for equal rights for blacks and married black Presbyterian minister Francis Grimké. Their home today is still a private residence but is one of the District of Columbia's seventy-five National Historic Landmarks. Penn School—known now as Penn Center—is also a National Historic Landmark and today is dedicated to preserving the history and heritage of Saint Helena and other coastal Sea Islands.

Booker T. Washington was born a slave on April 5, 1856, in Hale's Ford, Virginia. Perhaps no freed slave benefited more greatly from being educated than Washington. When the war ended, Washington moved to Malden, West Virginia, with his family and began working in a salt mine. Washington could neither read nor write, but he wrote years later that he had always dreamed of getting an education: "From the time that I can remember having any thoughts about anything, I recall that I had an intense longing to learn to read. I determined, when quite a small child, that, if I accomplished nothing else in life, I would in some way get enough education to enable me to read common books and newspapers."[43]

While working in the mines, Washington learned to recognize numbers written on barrels of salt. He then persuaded his mother to get him a book, and he began memorizing the alphabet. When a school opened, Washington's desire to learn was so strong that he attended night classes after working all day. Washington saved his money, and when he was sixteen he traveled alone to Richmond, Virginia, and enrolled in Hampton Institute, a school the American Missionary Association had founded in 1868 to train black teachers. Now known as Hampton University, it was designated a National Historic Landmark in 1974. The site includes a historic 98-foot-tall oak tree (29.9m) under which the Emancipation Proclamation in 1863 was read for the first time in a southern state. Known as the Emancipation Oak, the National Geographic Society has designated it one of the 10 Great Trees of the World.

Washington's teacher was William Davis, an educated free black from Ohio who had been a Union army cook. Teachers during the Reconstruction era included white and black southerners as well as many northerners, both white and black, who were sympathetic to the plight of the freed slaves. Even former slaves became teachers. Isabella Gibbons once worked as a slave on the University of Virginia campus for one of the college's teachers. After learning to read and write, she began teaching in Louisa

# White Violence toward Black Education

Edmonia Highgate died October 16, 1870. A historical marker in Oak-wood Cemetery in Syracuse, New York, where she is buried hails her as a teacher and fighter for black civil rights. Highgate was born in 1844 in New York to freed slaves. After graduating from high school with honors, Highgate became principal of a black school in Binghamton, New York. In 1864 Highgate began teaching in Reconstruction schools the American Missionary Association (AMA) started in Norfolk, Virginia, and New Orleans. In Louisiana Highgate encountered the white violence that plagued many black schools from people who opposed educating blacks. During the New Orleans Riots of July 1866, whites attacked teachers and other northerners helping blacks. Highgate then began teaching in a rural area in Lafayette Parish, but violence followed her to her new school. On December 17, 1866, Highgate wrote a letter to an AMA official about the danger she encountered: "Twice I have been shot at in my room. Some of my night-school scholars have been shot but none killed. . . . The rebels here threatened to burn down the school and house in which I board before the first month was passed. Yet they have not materially harmed us."

Quoted in *Civil War Women Blog.* "Black History Month Biography: Teacher of Freed Slaves Edmonia Highgate." February 14, 2011. www.civilwarwomenblog.com/2011/02/edmonia-highgate.html.

**During the New Orleans riots of 1866, white southerners attacked white teachers who were helping to educate blacks.**

County, Virginia, on October 15, 1866. Gibbons once wrote that so many blacks wanted to learn that there was not enough space for all the students: "The schools are filled, but children still come to see if they can be admitted. I have sixty-three pupils."[44]

The tradition of blacks teaching blacks was a long and proud one. For nearly a century after the Civil War, southern segregation forced whites and blacks to attend separate schools and even colleges and universities.

## Black Colleges

Although the first black southern schools of higher education did not open until after the Civil War, the Institute for Colored Youth was established in 1837 in Cheyney, Pennsylvania. Known now as Cheyney University, it was the nation's first black college or university. One of many historical markers about the school explains that in 1869 Fanny Jackson Coppin, who was born a slave in Washington, D.C., became the first woman, black or white, to head a coeducational school of higher learning. Black colleges that opened in the South during Reconstruction include Lincoln Normal School (now Alabama State University) in Marion, Alabama, in 1865; Barber-Scotia in Concord, North Carolina, in 1867, the first black college for women; and Howard University in Washington, D.C., in 1867. Lincoln Institute (now Lincoln University) in Jefferson City, Missouri, began in 1866 with an endowment of six thousand dollars from members of the Sixty-Second and Sixty-Fifth U.S. Colored Infantries.

Because most freed slaves had little or no formal schooling, those institutions of higher learning had to educate students in the basics of reading and writing before they could let them take more advanced classes. Many schools specialized in training teachers because there was such a great need for them. But on July 4, 1881, a new school opened with a different idea about what skills and education blacks needed to be successful. The founder of the Tuskegee Normal School for Colored Teachers— known now as Tuskegee University—was Booker T. Washington.

Although Washington was only twenty-five years old, he quickly made the school in Tuskegee, Alabama, successful by also teaching students how to become skilled carpenters, printers, and farmers as well as teachers, ministers, and businesspeople. Wash-

Tuskegee University, founded by Booker T. Washington, opened its doors in 1881. In 1965 the entire school was named a National Historic Landmark to honor its founder's work.

ington once said, "The Negro has the right to study law, but success will come to the race sooner if it produces intelligent, thrifty farmers, mechanics, to support the lawyers."[45] Washington's emphasis on industrial education attracted wealthy backers like John D. Rockefeller, and their donations helped him expand the school and even begin offering classes to people in rural areas as well as on the Tuskegee campus.

Washington's pioneer work in black higher education leadership made him the most prominent African American in the second half of the nineteenth century and Tuskegee the most famous black school. In 1965 the school was named a National Historic Landmark to honor the work Washington did.

Another famous African American educator was Mary McLeod Bethune, founder of Bethune-Cookman University in Daytona Beach, Florida. Bethune was born July 10, 1875, in Mayesville, South Carolina. She learned to read and write in a one-room schoolhouse and became a teacher after attending Dwight L. Moody's Institute for Home and Foreign Missions in Chicago. In 1904 she started the Literary and Industrial Training School for Negro Girls in Daytona.

Eight years later Washington advised her to seek contributions from wealthy whites, as he had. The donations Bethune received in following his advice helped her expand the school, and in 1920 it became the Daytona Normal and Industrial Institute. Three years later she merged it with Cookman Institute for Men in Jacksonville, Florida, to create Bethune-Cookman. In addition to being a noted educator, Bethune is famous for fighting for black civil rights and being an adviser to President Franklin D. Roosevelt. Many sites honor Bethune, including the Mary McLeod Bethune Memorial in Lincoln Park in Washington, D.C., which features a larger-than-life bronze statue of her. It was dedicated in 1974 by the National Council of Negro Women, which she founded in 1935.

## Why Educate Blacks?

Washington was a revered educator and black leader until he died on November 14, 1915. But before his death another legendary black leader—William Edward Burghardt (W.E.B.) Du Bois—challenged Washington's rationale for educating African Americans. Washington, a former slave, thought blacks should be educated as teachers and skilled workers. Du Bois, however, was born in Massachusetts three years after slavery ended. He attended Fisk University in Nashville, a black college, but in 1895 became the first African American to earn a doctorate degree from Harvard University. Du Bois believed blacks should also study to become lawyers, scientists, and government leaders.

Their division in opinion was based on their attitudes about how fast blacks should seek equality with whites. Washington wanted blacks to go slowly and believed they had to prove to whites over time that they were worthy of equality with them. Washington wrote:

> The wisest among my race understand that the agitation of questions of social equality is the extremest folly, and that progress in the enjoyment of all the privileges that will come to us must be the result of severe and constant struggle rather than of artificial forcing. It is important and right that all privileges of the law be ours, but it is vastly more important that we be prepared for the exercise of these privileges. The opportunity to earn a dollar in a factory just now is worth infinitely more than the opportunity to spend a dollar in an opera-house.[46]

W.E.B. Du Bois's boyhood home in Great Barrington, Massachusetts, was demolished long ago, but the ground it stood on has been designated a National Historic Landmark.

Du Bois was much more militant and wanted blacks to demand whites begin treating them as equals right away. He was a cofounder in 1909 of the National Association for the Advancement of Colored People (NAACP), the historic group that helped lead the civil rights fight in the twentieth century. Du Bois once wrote:

> We claim for ourselves every single right that belongs to a freeborn American, political, civil and social; and until we get these rights we will never cease to protest and assail the ears of America. The battle we wage is not for ourselves alone but for all true Americans. It is a fight for ideals, lest this, our common fatherland, false to its founding, become in truth the land of the thief and the home of the slave.[47]

Historic landmarks today honor both men, including the home in Great Barrington, Massachusetts, where Du Bois grew up. Although the home has been demolished, the site is a National Historic Landmark. The split between Washington and Du Bois about how fast blacks should gain equality was mirrored throughout black society. During the twentieth century Du Bois's stance prevailed, and blacks began fighting for the equality they knew they deserved.

## Chapter Five

# The Civil Rights Movement

After the Civil War, Republicans who controlled Congress proposed and states ratified three amendments to the U.S. Constitution to ensure that freed slaves would be treated equally with whites. The Thirteenth Amendment in 1865 abolished slavery. The Fourteenth Amendment in 1868 guaranteed citizenship and equal rights under the law to all people born in the United States except Native Americans, who would not win that right until 1924. And the Fifteenth Amendment in 1870 said the right to vote could not be denied by race, color, or previous condition of servitude.

But in the late 1870s southern states began passing laws that segregated the races, even though such laws violated the constitutional rights guaranteed blacks by the Thirteenth, Fourteenth, and Fifteenth Amendments. An example was in 1890 when a Louisiana law prohibited blacks from riding in train cars with whites. A New Orleans civil rights group persuaded black shoemaker Homer A. Plessy to buy a ticket on a white car to test the law's legality. After Plessy was arrested on June 7, 1892, the group appealed his conviction on the grounds that the law violated Plessy's Fourteenth Amendment rights to equal treatment under the law with whites. When Judge John Howard Ferguson ruled the law had not denied him his rights, the group appealed the decision to the U.S. Supreme Court.

On May 18, 1896, justices upheld Ferguson's decision and said states could create separate public facilities such as train cars for blacks and whites if they were equal in quality. The decision legalized more than six decades of racist laws southern states used to segregate the races. Blacks could not enter public places reserved for whites, such as restaurants, hotels, schools, bathrooms, or movie theaters. Southern states also passed laws that denied blacks rights like voting. This segregation became known as Jim Crow.

Today there is a historical marker in New Orleans near the site where Plessy was arrested. The marker was dedicated on February 11, 2009, with the help of descendants of both Plessy and Ferguson. Phoebe Ferguson said at the dedication, "That a part of my family started Jim Crow is kind of a load to carry. I wish I

Keith Plessy and Phoebe Ferguson, descendants of the principals in *Plessy v. Ferguson,* pose in front of the historical marker in New Orleans commemorating the place where Homer Plessy was arrested. The marker was dedicated on February 11, 2009.

could change that."[48] Although the decision today is considered racist, it was the law of the land until 1954, when a second Supreme Court decision overturned it.

## Brown v. Board of Education

Jim Crow allowed whites to dominate southern blacks economically and politically by denying them rights and legal protections the Constitution guaranteed them. Southern states were able to do that because federal officials and courts declined to protect the constitutional rights of African Americans. That changed in 1954 when the Supreme Court intervened to help blacks in a historic ruling that declared public school segregation illegal.

In the early 1950s seventeen states operated separate school systems for blacks and whites. The schools were separate but nev-

The *Brown v. Board of Education* National Historic Site in Topeka, Kansas, was dedicated on October 26, 1992. The site includes Monroe Elementary, the white school that refused to admit black students.

er equal in quality despite that requirement being handed down in the Supreme Court's *Plessy v. Ferguson* decision. White government officials never funded black schools equally with white schools, which meant blacks received inferior educations. By the end of 1952, blacks in Kansas, Delaware, the District of Columbia, South Carolina, and Virginia had asked the U.S. Supreme Court to rule on lawsuits challenging the constitutionality of school segregation. The high court chose *Brown v. Board of Education of Topeka* as its test case.

The NAACP had filed a class action lawsuit on behalf of parents like Oliver Brown who had tried to enroll their children in Monroe Elementary, a white school in Topeka, Kansas. On May 17, 1954, the Supreme Court ruled that segregated schools were unconstitutional in a decision that overturned the *Plessy v. Ferguson* decision that had justified segregation. The court ruled that "in the field of public education the doctrine of 'separate but equal' has no place [because segregation] of white and colored children in public schools has a detrimental effect upon the colored children."[49]

The high court ruling was historic because it was the first time the federal government had acted to end racial segregation in the South. On October 26, 1992, Congress established the *Brown v. Board of Education* National Historic Site in Topeka. The site includes Monroe Elementary, the white school that refused to admit black students, and it educates people about the role Monroe played in the fight for black rights.

The powerful new federal backing for their cause emboldened southern blacks in their long battle for legal equality with whites. A year after the high court decision, a black woman in Montgomery, Alabama, named Rosa Parks took the first brave step in what became known as the modern civil rights movement.

## Rosa Parks Defies Jim Crow

A historical marker at a bus stop and a library and museum in downtown Montgomery are named after Rosa Parks in honor of the courageous stand she took against racism on December 1, 1955. The marker reads simply, "At the bus stop on this site [Parks] refused to give up her seat to boarding whites."[50] Her refusal was an act of defiance because a 1945 Alabama law required

At the Henry Ford Museum in Dearborn, Michigan, President Barack Obama sits on the bus where Rosa Parks refused to give up her seat to a white man on December 1, 1955, in Montgomery, Alabama.

blacks to sit in the rear of buses and surrender their seats to whites if there were no empty seats. It was also an act of bravery because Parks knew she would be arrested. Years later Parks said she decided to fight racial injustice because of the brutal slaying a few months earlier of fourteen-year-old Emmett Till. While visiting family members in Money, Mississippi, the Chicago teenager had been murdered on August 28 because he whistled at a white woman. Whites had used such violence since the end of the Civil War to keep blacks afraid of them. Parks said Till's death made her angry enough to act: "We [had] finally reached the point where we [blacks] had to take action. I thought of Emmett Till and I couldn't [get up]."[51]

The arrest of Parks infuriated Montgomery blacks, and they began a boycott of the bus system to demand equal treatment with whites. The NAACP also filed a lawsuit that claimed the bus law was unconstitutional. On November 13, 1956, the Supreme

Court ruled that the law denied blacks their civil rights, and the court struck down the law to give blacks another major victory against racism. Parks has been honored for her decision to fight racism. On April 19, 2012, Barack Obama visited the Henry Ford Museum in Dearborn, Michigan, which has an exhibit about Parks that includes the bus in which she was arrested. After sitting in the bus and contemplating what Parks had done, Obama talked about why her act was important: "I just sat there for a moment and pondered the courage and tenacity that is part of our very recent history, but is also a part of that long line of folks—sometimes nameless, oftentimes didn't make the history books—but who constantly insisted on their dignity."[52]

Parks was not the only African American the boycott made a hero. Montgomery blacks chose Martin Luther King Jr., pastor of Dexter Avenue Baptist Church, to lead the boycott. The national

## Medgar Evers

---

Medgar Evers was an African American World War II veteran and civil rights activist. He was shot to death by a member of the Ku Klux Klan on June 12, 1963, after getting out of his car in the driveway of his home in Jackson, Mississippi. Ever's death received global media attention because he died shortly after President John F. Kennedy delivered a major television speech supporting black rights. Evers became one of the most revered martyrs of the civil rights movement because of his bravery in fighting racism. He has been honored in many ways since his death. On June 19 the navy veteran was buried with full military honors in Arlington National Cemetery. The city of Jackson erected a statue of Evers, named part of U.S. Highway 40 after him, and renamed the city airport Jackson-Evers International Airport. On November 12, 2011, the U.S. Navy christened a cargo ship the USNS *Medgar Evers*. Evers's finest legacy, however, is that his death strengthened the civil rights movement. There were only 28,000 black registered voters when he died, but by 1971 there were 250,000 and by 1982 more than 500,000. They helped elect black officials, including his brother Charles, who on May 13, 1969, became mayor of Fayetteville, Mississippi.

media coverage King received for his skillful handling of the situation made him one of the nation's most recognized and respected black leaders.

## Martin Luther King Jr.

King was only twenty-six years old when he led the boycott. Despite his youth, King's charismatic personality and eloquence in explaining why blacks were justified in challenging racial injustice made him a towering figure in the fight for civil rights. King's dramatic speeches inspired other blacks to fight racism and won millions of new white supporters for their cause. On August 28, 1963, King delivered his most famous speech to a crowd of 250,000 people in Washington, D.C.

His speech was delivered from the steps of the Lincoln Memorial. On October 16, 2011, not far from where King had spoken those words forty-eight years earlier, the Martin Luther King Jr. Memorial was dedicated. It is in the National Mall area, along with monuments honoring some of the nation's greatest heroes, including Abraham Lincoln, George Washington, and Thomas Jefferson. The centerpiece of his monument is a towering image of King carved from a huge slab of white granite 30 feet (9.1m) high. It was named the Stone of Hope in honor of the inspiration King provided to the civil rights movement. The 4-acre memorial (1.6ha) includes a wall 45 feet (140m) long bearing inscriptions of King's most famous speeches. Obama said at the dedication of the memorial: "In this place, he will stand for all time among monuments to those who fathered this nation and those who defended it; a black preacher with no official rank or title who somehow gave voice to our deepest dreams and our most lasting ideals, a man who stirred our conscience and thereby helped make our union more perfect."[53]

The memorial honors King not only for his words but for his courageous actions in fighting racism. King was arrested and jailed several times for leading protests, and he was often targeted for violence by racist whites. During the Montgomery bus boycott, his home was bombed. King was not home at the time, and neither his wife nor children were injured. He continued to receive death threats from whites angry that he was trying to help blacks win equality. On April 4, 1968, those threats became reality when King was shot to death in Memphis, Tennessee, while standing on the balcony of the Lorraine Motel. Today the motel is part of the National Civil Rights Museum, which traces the history of civil rights from the seventeenth century to the present.

The Memphis museum and the memorial in the nation's capital are only two of many historic sites and landmarks honoring King. However, tens of thousands of people, black and white, were jailed, beaten, and killed in the fight to give blacks equality with whites. And today hundreds of historic landmarks honor and celebrate what they did.

The Martin Luther King Jr. Memorial on the National Mall in Washington, D.C., was dedicated on October 16, 2011. It features a towering image of King sculpted in white granite.

## Fannie Lou Hamer

The Fannie Lou Hamer Memorial Garden in Ruleville, Mississippi, honors one of the state's most revered civil rights heroes. Hamer was born on October 6, 1917, in Montgomery County, Mississippi. By age six she was picking cotton, and she quit school after the sixth grade to work full-time. In 1962 Hamer tried to register to vote. Even though she was arrested and not allowed to register, the white owner of the plantation where she worked fired her and threatened Hamer by saying, "We're not going to have this in Mississippi." Instead of being intimidated, Hamer became a field worker for the Student Nonviolent Coordinating Committee. Hamer once said that she ignored what whites might do to her: "I guess if I'd had any sense I'd a-been a little scared, but what was the point of being scared? The only thing they could do to me was kill me and it seemed like they'd been trying to do that a little bit at a time ever since I could remember." On June 9, 1963, Hamer was arrested again and beaten severely. But she kept on protesting and helped blacks win the right to vote.

Quoted in Dorothy R. Abbott, ed. *Mississippi Writers: Reflections of Childhood and Youth.* Jackson: University Press of Mississippi, 1985, p. 322.

## Fighting Jim Crow

In 1960 when fast food restaurants were far less ubiquitous than they are today, millions of people ate inexpensive meals at lunch counters in department or drug stores. Southern blacks could shop in those stores but not eat there, because food service was reserved for whites. On February 1, 1960, four students from North Carolina Agricultural and Technical College challenged that segregation by sitting down and ordering food at the F.W. Woolworth Company store in Greensboro, North Carolina. Even though a waitress told them, "We don't serve colored here,"[54] they stayed until the store closed. They returned the next day with twenty more students to again demand service, and eventually the number of protesters involved in the continuing protest at other lunch counters in the South grew to more than one thousand.

In the next year more than seventy thousand people used the peaceful sit-in tactic pioneered by Franklin McCain, Joseph Mc-

Neil, Ezell Blair Jr., and David Richmond to protest restaurant segregation. Four thousand people were arrested, but the protests were so powerful that restaurant owners in 119 southern cities began serving blacks. A fitting tribute to those historic protests is that the Woolworth store building where the first sit-in was held today houses the International Civil Rights Center & Museum.

Sit-ins marked the first time large numbers of high school and college students joined the fight for civil rights. In the spring of 1961, adults and college students took black protest in a new direction by becoming Freedom Riders. Although the Montgomery bus boycott had ended segregation in local bus service, buses traveling between states still enforced segregated seating. On May 4 two groups of riders that included black and white protesters left Washington, D.C., on Greyhound and Trailways buses bound

**Visitors to the International Civil Rights Center & Museum in the former Woolworth's building in Greensboro, North Carolina, sit at the same lunch counter where four black students challenged restaurant segregation with a sit-in on February 1, 1960.**

for New Orleans. In the Alabama cities of Anniston and Montgomery, racist whites attacked riders for sitting together on the bus and sharing the whites-only bathrooms. The worst incident occurred on May 20, when twenty-one riders reached Montgomery. Whites wielding ax-handles and pipes beat protesters as they got off the bus.

Today that bus station in downtown Montgomery houses the Freedom Riders Museum, a historic site that educates people about racism. The protests received national news coverage, and the brave actions of Freedom Riders eventually forced the federal government to ban segregation on interstate buses.

White private citizens and law enforcement officials had always used violence to stop blacks from fighting Jim Crow. This violence was never more brutal or bloody than when blacks began to fight for the right to vote.

The Freedom Riders Museum in Montgomery, Alabama, is housed in the former Greyhound Bus building and was opened to the public in June 2011.

## The Right to Vote

Racist whites feared that if blacks gained the right to vote, whites would lose political power because there would be so many black voters. For nearly a century whites had denied blacks the right to vote, a tactic called disenfranchisement, so whites could retain power over African Americans. When civil rights protests in the early 1960s shifted to winning voting rights, whites did everything possible to stop that from happening. On July 26, 1962, Terrell County sheriff Z.T. Matthews broke up a peaceful voter registration rally at Mount Olive Baptist Church in Sasser, Georgia. Matthews then told a reporter why he had acted: "We want our colored people to go on living like they have for the last hundred years."[55] Matthews knew that if blacks were able to vote, they would be able to elect officials, including other blacks, who would treat them fairly.

Black and white volunteers, including many from northern states, worked hard in the next few years to register voters, but violence and resistance by southern whites kept them from making much progress. An example of this violence occurred on August 31, 1961, when Robert Moses was brutally beaten for trying to register voters in Liberty, Mississippi. The lack of success led King in 1965 to lead a historic protest in Selma, Alabama, that finally forced the federal government to intervene to help blacks.

The Selma protest lasted several weeks and was supposed to culminate on March 7 with a protest march from Selma to Montgomery. But that day state and local law enforcement officials armed with clubs and tear gas attacked six hundred men, women, and children who were peacefully marching out of town over the Edmund Pettus Bridge. The violence was recorded by news crews with television cameras and was so brutal that the city earned the nickname "Bloody Selma." Weeks later, on March 21, marchers who were now protected by federal law enforcement officials walked over the Pettus Bridge. Four days later they arrived in Montgomery and held a triumphant rally to celebrate the successful march; the rally included a powerful speech by King.

National outrage over the Selma violence forced President Lyndon B. Johnson to introduce the 1965 Voting Rights Act. On August 6 Congress passed the bill, which allowed the federal government to monitor elections and make sure southern blacks could

# Foot Soldiers Monument

The Foot Soldiers Monument in the Plaza de la Constitución in Saint Augustine, Florida, honors people from that city, both black and white, who helped African Americans win their civil rights. The 675-pound bronze sculpture (306kg) depicts four people standing shoulder to shoulder in front of a relief that illustrates a civil rights protest. The monument was dedicated on May 14, 2011. A plaque describes the many types of protests and sacrifices people made to win black rights. Although the words refer to people and protests in Saint Augustine, they can be applied equally to honor tens of thousands of anonymous people who fought for civil rights:

> Dedicated to those who participated in the Civil Rights Movement of the 1960s. . . . They protested racial discrimination by marching, picketing, kneeling-in at churches, sitting-in at lunch counters, wading-in at beaches, attending rallies, raising money, preparing meals and providing a safe haven.
>
> They persisted in the face of jailings, beatings, shootings, loss of employment, threats, and other dangers. They were Foot Soldiers for Freedom and Justice. . . .
>
> Their courage and heroism changed America and inspired the world.

Quoted in Waymarking. "St. Augustine Foot Soldiers Monument—St. Augustine, FL." www.waymarking.com/waymarks/WMDKZC_St_Augustine_Foot_Soldiers_Monument_St_Augustine_FL.

The Foot Soldiers Monument In St. Augustine, Florida, honors the city's residents who helped African Americans gain their civil rights.

vote. The resulting political power that southern blacks won finally gave them a true measure of equality with whites.

Many historic landmarks honor the historic protest. One of the most significant came in 1996 when Congress designated the 54-mile route (87km) marchers walked as the Selma-to-Montgomery March National Historic Trail. The historic trail includes the bridge, which has a central span of 250 feet (76m) and was built in 1940.

During the civil rights movement, many peaceful protests turned violent when protesters were attacked. As such, there are many other landmarks honoring people who fought and died so that African Americans' civil rights would be protected.

## They Gave Their Lives

A marker near Philadelphia, Mississippi, bears the names of James Chaney, Andrew Goodman and Michael "Mickey" Schwerner. In the summer of 1965 the three men—Chaney, a black from Meridian, Mississippi, and Goodman and Schwerner, white northerners—were helping blacks register to vote. On June 21 a Neshoba County deputy who knew they were civil rights workers arrested them for allegedly speeding. Deputies then turned the civil rights workers over to Ku Klux Klan members, who shot them to death. A headstone monument at Mount Nebo Missionary Baptist Church in Jackson, Mississippi, near where they were killed is one of many historic sites that honor them.

Viola Liuzzo was a civil rights activist from Detroit who helped in the Selma voting rights protest. On March 25, 1965, Ku Klux Klan members shot Liuzzo to death while she was driving march participants home from Montgomery. In 1991 the Women of the Southern Christian Leadership Conference honored her with a marker on Highway 80 near where she was killed. The Viola Liuzzo Memorial says simply, "In memory of our sister Viola Liuzzo who gave her life in the struggle for the right to vote."[56]

# Chapter Six

# African American Achievers

**B**ritish colonists justified enslaving blacks in the seventeenth century by claiming they were inferior to whites mentally, emotionally, and physically. It did not take long, however, before slaves like Phillis Wheatley and others proved they could equal or surpass the achievements of whites when given the opportunity. Wheatley was born in 1753 in Gambia-Senegal. She was sold into slavery and taken to Boston, where John Wheatley bought her in August 1761 as a servant for his wife, Susanna. The couple named her Phillis after the ship that transported her from Africa, and they gave her their last name. The Wheatleys educated Phillis, and in a period when many whites were illiterate, she learned to read and write in English, Latin, and Greek.

Phillis began writing poetry, and in 1773 the Wheatleys helped her publish *Poems on Various Subjects, Religious and Moral*. Her book was published in England because no colonial printer would publish a black author. When Wheatley's poems had been printed in newspapers before that, so many whites doubted she had written them that in 1772 she was forced to defend her literary ability. In a meeting with several well-known Massachusetts people, including Governor Thomas Hutchinson and John Hancock, whose signature would become famous four years later when he signed the Declaration of Independence,

Wheatley proved to them she had written the poems. They signed a statement acknowledging Wheatley was the author, and it was included in her book of poetry.

Wheatley understood why whites doubted her ability to write poetry. In "On Being Brought from Africa to America," she addressed the topic of whether blacks could achieve as much as whites:

Twas mercy brought me from my Pagan land,
Taught my benighted soul to understand,
That there's a God, that there's a Saviour too:
Once I redemption neither sought nor knew.
Some view our sable race with scornful eye,
"Their colour is a diabolic die."
Remember, Christians, Negros, black as Cain,
May be refin'd and join the angelic train.[57]

Wheatley was freed from slavery in 1778 but died in poverty on December 5, 1784. She had written another book of poetry, but no one would publish it; the only job she could get was as a maid.

The Boston Women's Memorial Common is the site of many figures of women who fought to abolish slavery. The bronze statue of Phillis Wheatley shown here commemorates the first African American woman to publish a book of poetry.

Wheatley was buried in an unmarked grave but has been honored in many ways since then. The most impressive monument is a statue in the Boston Women's Memorial Common, which includes figures of First Lady Abigail Adams and Lucy Stone, who fought to abolish slavery and secure the right of women to vote. The bronze statue, which depicts Wheatley leaning on a massive marble block as if contemplating writing a poem, was dedicated on October 25, 2003. Sculptor Meredith Bergmann explained why Wheatley's achievements were impressive: "External, legal freedom was denied to Phillis Wheatley. But she sought the inner freedom that enabled her to write. . . . Her words, her letters grow on us because democracy requires that we continue shining light upon our past mistakes, especially the sin of slavery. Her triumph is the freedom that she found and recognized within herself."[58]

## Toni Morrison's Bench

Some of the most famous black writers are Langston Hughes, Richard Wright, James Baldwin, Zora Neale Hurston, and Alice Walker. One of the most honored is Toni Morrison, whose novel *Beloved* is based on the true story of an escaped slave named Margaret who killed her two-year-old daughter rather than have her returned to slavery. Morrison won the Nobel Prize in 1993 and *Beloved* was awarded the Pulitzer Prize in 1987. In 1989 Morrison said she wrote *Beloved* because there are few historical markers honoring slaves: "There is no suitable memorial, or plaque, or wreath, or wall, or park, or skyscraper lobby. There's no 300-foot tower, there's no small bench by the road. . . . And because such a place doesn't exist the book had to." On February 18, 2006, the Toni Morrison Society and the National Park Service placed a bench on Sullivan's Island, South Carolina, the arrival point for many slaves. The bench has a plaque that explains people should sit on the bench and remember them. The society's Bench by the Road Project planned to install benches at other locations selected from Morrison's novels and of historical significance to African Americans.

Quoted in Toni Morrison Society. "Bench by the Road Project." www.tonimorrisonsociety.org/bench.html.

Wheatley was the first African American woman to publish a book of poetry. Since then many other blacks have achieved great things to rival her feat. Important among them were early black scientists and inventors who disproved racial theories that claimed blacks lacked intelligence.

## Brilliant Black Minds

The Benjamin Banneker Historical Park and Museum in Baltimore honors the man who was the colonial period's most celebrated African American. The park includes a replica of the log cabin in which Banneker lived and worked most of his life. Banneker was born free in Ellicott Mills, Maryland, on November 9, 1731. He received only a rudimentary education but studied on his own to become a mathematician, scientist, and author known for his fine intellect. Banneker used his knowledge of astronomy and mathematics to predict solar and lunar eclipses and publish almanacs filled with scientific and medical knowledge, including times the sun would rise and set each day. Banneker also helped architect Pierre Charles L'Enfant survey streets for Washington, D.C. The National Park Service created a small park in Banneker's honor there that includes a boundary stone he laid that is a National Historic Landmark.

Thomas Jefferson knew Banneker and had recommended him to L'Enfant. But on August 19, 1791, Banneker wrote Jefferson a letter that criticized him for owning slaves and accused him of believing blacks were inferior intellectually even though he had written in the Declaration of Independence that all men were created equal. Banneker asked Jefferson's help "to eradicate that train of absurd and false ideas and opinions, which so generally prevails with respect to us [blacks] and [to make people realize that God] hath not only made us all of one flesh, but that he hath also . . . endowed us all with the same faculties."[59]

As proof of his own intelligence, Banneker sent Jefferson a copy of his first almanac. In his reply on August 30, Jefferson, then secretary of state, wrote, "No body wishes more than I do to see such proofs as you exhibit, that nature has given to our black brethren, talents equal to those of the other colors of men." Jefferson wrote that he had sent Banneker's almanac to a French scientist "because I considered it as a document to which your

A statue of a youthful George Washington Carver looks over a walking path at the George Washington Carver National Monument near Carver's birthplace in Diamond, Missouri. Dedicated in 1943, it was the first national monument for an American who had not been president.

whole colour had a right for their justification against the doubts which have been entertained of them."[60]

George Washington Carver National Monument in Diamond, Missouri, celebrates the life of the most famous African American scientist. Dedicated on July 14, 1943, just six months after Carver died, it was the first national monument for someone who had not been president. Franklin D. Roosevelt donated thirty thousand dollars to the creation of the monument. The monument preserves the farm where Carver was born a slave in 1864, his boyhood home, and the woods and prairies he explored as a child. The site includes a statue of Carver as a young boy sitting on a rock and looking upward as if he is investigating the trees that surround it. That pose is symbolic of Carver's love of plants and his desire to learn as much about them as he could.

After the Civil War ended slavery, German immigrant Moses Carver, Washington's former master, adopted Washington, who went from being known as "Carver's George" to George Carver. The young boy graduated from high school and went to Iowa State Agricultural College (now Iowa State), where he earned a master's degree in botany. In 1896 Carver was named head of the Agriculture Department at Tuskegee Institute, where he taught for forty-seven years. Carver became famous for his research in how to improve soil and more efficiently grow peanuts, soybeans, and sweet potatoes. Carver's celebrity as a scientist enabled him to preach racial harmony between whites and blacks. A plaque at his birthplace praises Carver as someone "who rose from slavery to become a distinguished scientist and a great force in creating racial understanding."[61]

Many nineteenth-century African American inventors also proved that the notion that black people were not as smart as whites was thoroughly misguided and completely incorrect. Thomas L. Jennings is the first African American awarded a patent for an invention. On March 3, 1822, the state of New York approved his idea for a cleaning process known as dry scouring, which is known today as dry cleaning. Jennings was a free black, but he used profits from his dry cleaning business to buy family members out of slavery.

The ideas of Garrett Augustus Morgan Sr., who was born March 4, 1877, in Paris, Kentucky, continue to have an even greater impact on life today. A historic marker dedicated in 2003 in Cleveland, where he lived most of his life, identifies Morgan as "an African American businessman and prolific inventor of devices that made people's lives safer and more convenient."[62] Morgan invented the traffic light, which makes travel safer for drivers and pedestrians, and a safety hood that used a wet sponge to filter smoke so firefighters could breathe while they rescued people.

These African Americans succeeded despite racism that made their lives harder. Other blacks found success in the world of entertainment.

# Inventor, Businessperson, Millionaire

A building in Indianapolis, Indiana, was named a National Historic Landmark in 1991 in honor of Madam C.J. Walker, who was the first African American woman to become a millionaire. The historic designation states the 1927 building "was the hub of the beauty industry initiated and developed by Madame C.J. Walker (1867–1919), the first Black woman to open the field of cosmetology as a new and lucrative industry for Black women. For years, the Walker Company was the most successful Black business in the United States." Walker invented hair care and beauty products for black women and became rich selling them throughout the United States. The Madam C.J. Walker Manufacturing Company in Indianapolis employed three thousand black women. Walker also fought for black civil rights and helped other black women start businesses. Walker was born Sarah Breedlove on December 23, 1867, in Delta, Louisiana. Her parents had been slaves, and she was their first child born after slavery ended. At the age of twenty, Walker moved to St. Louis, where three of her brothers were barbers, and began studying hair care. In 1906 she married Charles Joseph Walker and four years later moved to Indianapolis and opened her factory.

Quoted in National Historic Landmarks Program. "Madame C.J. Walker Manufacturing Company." http://tps.cr.nps.gov/nhl/detail.cfm?ResourceId=1817&ResourceType=Building.

C.J. Walker, the first female African American millionaire, sits behind the wheel of her car in 1916.

## Black Stars

The Delta Blues Museum in Clarksdale, Mississippi, explains the history of the blues, a style of music southern blacks originated in the early twentieth century that is the direct ancestor of rap and rock and roll. The museum is housed in the Yazoo and Mississippi Valley Passenger Depot, which was built in 1926. The depot was placed on the National Register of Historic Places in 1995 because of the role it played in spreading the blues. Blues artists like Muddy Waters departed from the depot for Chicago and other northern cities to escape southern racism. The music they carried with them, which had elements of African music that set it apart from other musical styles, quickly became popular among both blacks and whites.

The museum is part of the Mississippi Blues Trail, a series of historical sites and markers that traces the history of the blues and the role the music has played in shaping American culture. The trail includes a site in Chicago that was dedicated on June 11, 2009, because it is near an old train station that was the end point of the journey of tens of thousands of southern blacks who migrated north seeking better lives. Among them were blues greats like Willie Dixon, Memphis Minnie, Big Bill Broonzy, Howlin' Wolf, Bo Diddley, and B.B. King.

Although blues legend Robert Johnson wrote the classic song "Sweet Home Chicago," he never moved to Chicago. But Johnson's birthplace marker in Hazlehurst, Mississippi, notes, "His music struck a chord that continues to resonate. His blues addresses generations he never knew and made poetry of his vision and fears."[63] Even though Johnson died on August 16, 1938, recordings of his music inspired British blues and rock stars like Mick Jagger and Eric Clapton; in 2004 the latter recorded *Me and Mr. Johnson*, an album of Johnson's songs that was a tribute to Clapton's long-dead mentor.

Until the second half of the twentieth century, blues artists and other black performers usually had to perform in segregated nightclubs and theaters. The "Chitlin' Circuit" was a string of entertainment venues in northern and southern cities that hosted black acts. The circuit included the Apollo Theater in New York City, Regal Theater in Chicago, Fox Theatre in Detroit, and Carver Theatre in Birmingham, Alabama. Tyler Perry has performed

This tableau of blues icon Muddy Waters is part of the Delta Blues Museum in Clarksdale, Mississippi. In 1995 the museum was placed on the National Register of Historic Places for its role in spreading that music genre throughout America.

many of his plays in those theaters, and it was in Chicago's Regal Theater that he first played Madea, the zany, outspoken southern woman who is his most beloved character.

One of the most historic examples of such segregation involved Marian Anderson, who was born on February 27, 1897, and against all odds became one of the twentieth century's most celebrated opera singers. Despite being black, Anderson's magnificent voice had made her a major star in the United States and Europe by the late 1930s. In 1939, however, the Daughters of the American Revolution (DAR) refused to let her perform for an integrated audience in Constitution Hall, a concert hall in Washington, D.C., that they owned. The insult to Anderson caused First Lady Eleanor Roosevelt and thousands of women to resign from the DAR.

When Anderson was also denied use of a high school auditorium for the concert, Franklin D. Roosevelt arranged for her to sing on the steps of the Lincoln Memorial. The concert became a landmark event in the fight for black rights when a mixed-race crowd of seventy-five thousand turned out for her performance, which was also broadcast on radio to millions of people. Anderson wrote that despite being nervous, she understood how important it was for her to sing: "My Lord, What a Morning. I could see that my significance as an individual was small in this affair. I had become, whether I liked it or not, a symbol, representing my people. I had to appear."[64] Many other historical sites honor Anderson for her singing and her role in the civil rights movement, including the Marian Anderson Residence Museum in her native Philadelphia.

Paul Robeson was another concert singer and actor who suffered because of racism. Robeson was born on April 9, 1898, in Princeton, New Jersey. His father, William, was a slave who had

Singer, actor, athlete, and civil rights activist Paul Robeson has been honored by his alma mater, Rutgers University, by having several buildings named after him. His homes in Philadelphia and Manhattan have become National Historic Landmarks as well.

served in the Union army during the Civil War and afterward became a Presbyterian minister. Robeson graduated from Rutgers University and Columbia Law School, but his law career was brief because he realized racism would only allow him to do menial work as a lawyer. Robeson began an acting and singing career that made him one of the early twentieth century's most celebrated black entertainers. Robeson also worked tirelessly for black rights.

Since his death on January 23, 1976, Robeson has been honored in many ways. Rutgers University named several buildings after him, and his homes in Manhattan and Philadelphia are National Historic Landmarks. In addition, in 1995 Robeson was inducted into the College Football Hall of Fame. Robeson played four years for Rutgers on a powerful team that had a 22-6-3 record and outscored its opponents 941-191 in 31 games. But like many black athletes then, Robeson's most powerful opponent in sports was racism.

## Black Athletes Battle Racism

Robeson had a full academic scholarship to Rutgers but wanted to play football. When the seventeen-year-old freshman tried to make the team in the fall of 1915, white players brutalized him in his first practice because they did not want a black teammate. One player smashed Robeson's nose so hard that it bothered him the rest of his life, and another dislocated his right shoulder by kneeing him in the back while he was on the ground. It took Robeson ten days to recover from the injuries. Years later he explained why he decided to return to practice: "[My father] had impressed upon me that when I was out on a football field or in a classroom or anywhere else . . . I was the representative of a lot of Negro boys who wanted to play football and wanted to go to college, and, as their representative, I had to show that I could take whatever was handed out."[65]

When Robeson came back, his bravery and toughness forced the coach and players to accept him. As a defensive end and running back, Robeson was twice named an All-American, and he played professionally from 1920 to 1922 to pay his way through law school. Robeson was one of many athletes who suffered discrimination in breaking down racial barriers in sports. Although a few blacks played professional football in the 1920s and early 1930s,

## "Unforgivable Blackness"

———————————■———————————

Heavyweight boxing champions Joe Louis and Muhammad Ali are remembered and honored today by many historic landmarks. But there are few historical reminders of Jack Johnson, the first African American to win the title of world heavyweight boxing champion. John Arthur "Jack" Johnson was born on March 31, 1878, in Galveston, Texas, to former slaves Henry and Tina Johnson. On December 26, 1908, Johnson defeated Canadian Tommy Burns to win the title. Many whites were upset that an African American held the championship title, and finding a white boxer to beat Johnson became something of a national obsession. After several white boxers tried and failed to take the title from Johnson, former champion James J. Jeffries came out of retirement to fight Johnson. Whites were confident that Jeffries could beat Johnson and called him the "Great White Hope." On July 4, 1910, in Reno, Nevada, in what was called the "Fight of the Century," Johnson defeated Jeffries. The six-foot tall Johnson held the title for seven years. Today the only reminder of that historic fight is a small marker in Reno. Whites then hated Johnson for being a black champion and defying racial barriers by marrying three white women and refusing to be humble toward whites. In 1909 W.E.B. Du Bois wrote that "the reason Jack Johnson was so beset by his own country, a country ironically which had only recently reaffirmed that all men were created equal, was because of his Unforgivable Blackness." That comment is also probably the most likely explanation of why there are so few reminders today of what Johnson accomplished.

Quoted in Shelley Gabert. " Boxing While Black: Ken Burns Chronicles Jack Johnson's Bout with Racism." International Documentary Association, January 2005. www.documentary.org/content/boxing -while-black-ken-burns-chronicles-jack-johnsons-bout-racism.

the sport was officially segregated until March 21, 1946, when the Los Angeles Rams signed former University of California–Los Angeles star Kenny Washington. One year later Jackie Robinson broke the color barrier in the nation's most popular sport—baseball.

Jack Roosevelt Robinson debuted with the Brooklyn Dodgers on April 15, 1947, to become the first black major league player. Despite taunts from fans, opposing players, and even his own teammates, Robinson played so well that other teams began signing black players. Robinson was eventually elected to the Baseball

Hall of Fame and is one of the most honored athletes in the history of sports for breaking baseball's color barrier. The greatest honor accorded him happens every April 15, when every Major League Baseball player wears Robinson's number, 42, on his jersey for an entire game. That unusual tribute began in 2004, seven years after Major League Baseball retired his jersey; it was the first time a player's number was retired for every team in any sport instead of just that player's team.

The last player to wear 42 was Mariano Rivera. The New York Yankee pitcher was allowed to continue wearing it because it was his jersey number. On Jackie Robinson day in 2012, the Panama native said, "I'm honored to wear it, to use it. It's wonderful. As a minority, being the last one to use No. 42 is tremendous."[66] Many other black athletes have been honored since then for breaking

The Los Angeles Dodgers, all wearing number 42, line up on April 15, 2007, "Jackie Robinson Day," on which every major league ball player wears Robinson's number 42 in a living tribute. Robinson is the only player to have his number retired by every major league team.

racial barriers in sports, including Arthur Ashe in tennis and Tiger Woods in golf for giving blacks a chance to play every level of every sport.

## "A Space of Moral Principle"

Kirk Savage, an expert on the history of monuments, believes historic landmarks, monuments, and even simple plaques about people or achievements do not just recognize past history but serve as a comment on what happened. He also admits that landmarks can sometimes take on a life of their own. Savage said when Anderson sang at the Lincoln Memorial, her appearance in defiance of segregation transformed the already majestic National Mall area because "it was now a space of moral principle, designed by the citizens who occupied it."[67] And it is the moral underpinning of African American landmarks, namely the need to affirm the sacrifices and achievements blacks made in the past to secure a better future today, that truly makes them so important.

# Notes

## Introduction: The Importance of Landmarks

1. Quoted in Margaret Wappler. "Obamas Attend Groundbreaking for African American History Museum." *Los Angeles Times*, February 22, 2012. http://latimesblogs.latimes.com/cul turemonster/2012/02/obama-and -others-celebrate-construction-of -african-american-history-museum .html.

2. Thomas Carlyle. *Latter-Day Pamphlets by Thomas Carlyle*. Project Gutenberg, July 26, 2008. www.gutenberg.org /ebooks/1140.

3. Quoted in Diane Ravitch, ed. *The American Reader: Words That Moved a Nation*. New York: HarperPerennial, 1991, p. 140.

4. Quoted in Brett Zongker. "New Black History Museum Rising on D.C.'s National Mall." *Aiken (SC) Standard*, February 22, 2012. www .aikenstandard.com/story/V5180-AP -US-Smithsonian-Black-7thLd-Write thru-02-22-0785.

## Chapter One: The Slavery Era

5. Quoted in Christine Mullen Kream- er. "Crossroads of People, Cross- roads of Trade." *Museum News*, March/April 2007. www.aam-us.org /pubs/mn/crossroads.cfm.

6. Quoted in Michael Scherer. "Obama's Statement at Cape Coast Castle." *Time*, July 11, 2009. http://swamp land.time.com/2009/07/11/obamas -statement-at-cape-coast-castle.

7. Quoted in Lisa Rein. "Mystery of Va.'s First Slaves Is Unlocked 400 Years Later." *Washington Post*, September 3, 2006. www.washingtonpost.com /wp-dyn/content/article/2006/09/02 /AR2006090201097.html.

8. Quoted in Katherine Calos. "Oppor- tunity Lost at Jamestown." *Richmond (VA) Times-Dispatch*, May 15, 2007, p. 1.

9. Quoted in Eyre Crowe. *With Thac- keray in America*. London: Cassell, 1893, p. 130. http://historymatters .gmu.edu/d/6762.

10. Quoted in Library of Congress. "Creat- ing the Declaration of Independence." http://myloc.gov/Exhibitions/Creating theUS/interactives/declaration/HTML /equal/index.html.

11. Quoted in Jim Davenport. "Slave Memorial Abuts Confederate Flag." *Los Angeles Times*, March 25, 2001. http://articles.latimes.com/2001/mar /25/news/mn-42336.

12. Quoted in Paul Aron. *Mysteries in History: From Prehistory to the Pres- ent*. Santa Barbara, CA: ABC-Clio, 2005, p. 213.

13. Quoted in AfricaWithin.com. "Crispus Attucks." www.africawithin.com/bios/crispus_attucks.htm.

14. Quoted in Find a Grave. "Jeff Liberty." www.findagrave.com/cgi-bin/fg.cgi?page=gr&GRid=50829351.

15. Quoted in Jeffrey J. Crow. "'Liberty to Slaves': The Black Response." *Tar Heel Junior Historian*, Fall 1992, p. 19. www.learnnc.org/lp/editions/nchist-revolution/1917.

16. Quoted in Beckwourth Trail: A Route to the Gold Country. "Discovery of the Beckwourth Trail." www.beckwourth.org/Trail/discovery.html.

17. Quoted in KVIE Public Television. "African Americans in California's Heartland." www.kvie.org/programs/kvie/viewfinder/africanamericans/transcript.swf.

18. Quoted in Historical Marker Database. "Moses Rodgers Home, 1890." www.hmdb.org/marker.asp?marker=23973.

19. Quoted in Erica Brown. "Congress Honors Slaves Who Built United States Capitol." *Cincinnati Herald*, February 12, 2011. www.thecincinnatiherald.com/news/2011-02-12/News/Congress_honors_slaves_who_built_United_States_Cap.html.

## Chapter Two: African Americans Resist Slavery

20. Lerone Bennett Jr. *Before the Mayflower: A History of Black America.* New York: Penguin, 1988, p. 111.

21. Howard Jones. "Slave Mutiny on the Amistad." *American History*, February 1998. www.historynet.com/slave-mutiny-on-the-amistad.htm.

22. Quoted in U.S. 17 Coastal Highway. "Historical Markers: Stono Rebellion Historical Marker." www.us17coastalhighway.com/historical-markers.

23. Quoted in David Slade. "Groundbreaking for Vesey Monument." *Charleston (SC) Post and Courier*, February 20, 2010. www.postandcourier.com/article/20100202/PC1602/302029944.

24. Frederick Douglass. *The Frederick Douglass Papers: Series One; Speeches, Debates, and Interviews.* Vol. 1. New Haven, CT: Yale University Press, 1979. p. 398.

25. Quoted in Andrew Malcolm. "Sojourner Truth Becomes First Black Woman to Be Honored Among Statues at U.S. Capitol." *Los Angeles Times*, April 28, 2009. http://latimesblogs.latimes.com/washington/2009/04/sojourner-truth-becomes-first-female-bust-installed-in-us-capitol-with-help-from-first-lady-michelle.html.

26. Quoted in New York State Office of Parks, Recreation, & Historic Preservation. "John Brown Farm State Historic Site." http://nysparks.com/historic-sites/29/details.aspx.

## Chapter Three: The Civil War

27. Quoted in National Park Service. "The Great Emancipator." www.nps.gov/linc/index.htm.

28. Abraham Lincoln. "Transcript of Gettysburg Address (1863)." Our Documents. www.ourdocuments.gov/doc.php?doc=36&page=transcript.

29. Abraham Lincoln. "House Divided Speech, 1858." Digital History. www.digitalhistory.uh.edu/documents/documents_p2.cfm?doc=26.

30. Quoted in National Park Service. "Living Contraband —Former Slaves in the Nation's Capital During the Civil War." www.nps.gov/cwdw/historyculture/living-contraband-former-slaves-in-the-capital-during-and-after-the-civil-war.htm.

31. Frederick Douglass. "The Work of the Future." *Douglass' Monthly*, November 1862. www.lib.rochester.edu/index.cfm?PAGE=4405.

32. Quoted in Samuel Eliot Morison. *The Oxford History of the American People*. New York: Oxford University Press, 1965, p. 653.

33. Quoted in National Archives. "Teaching with Documents: The Fight for Equal Rights; Black Soldiers in the Civil War." www.archives.gov/education/lessons/blacks-civil-war.

34. Quoted in Kirk Savage. *Standing Soldiers, Kneeling Slaves: Race, War, and Monument in Nineteenth-Century America*. Princeton, NJ: Princeton University Press, 1997, p. 203.

35. Quoted in Liberty Letters. "Harriet Tubman: Civil War Spy, Daring Soldier." http://libertyletters.com

/resources/civil-war/harriet-tubman-civil-war-spy.php.

36. *Boston Commonwealth*. "Campaign on the Combahee." July 10, 1863. www.harriettubman.com/tubman2.html.

37. Quoted in Earl Conrad. *Harriet Tubman: Negro Soldier and Abolitionist*. New York: International, p. 40.

38. Kirk Savage. *Monument Wars: Washington, D.C., the National Mall, and the Transformation of the Memorial Landscape*. Berkeley: University of California Press, 2005, p. 8.

## Chapter Four: Education for Blacks

39. Frederick Douglass. *Life and Times of Frederick Douglass*. Documenting the American South, 2001. http://docsouth.unc.edu/neh/dougl92/dougl92.html.

40. Quoted in Markeroni. "Historical Marker Transcription." www.markeroni.com/catalog/display.php?code=ON_NR_02015.

41. Henry Bibb. *Narrative of the Life and Adventures of Henry Bibb, an American Slave, Written by Himself*. Documenting the American South, 2000. http://docsouth.unc.edu/neh/bibb/bibb.html.

42. Quoted in William Loren Katz. *Eyewitness: The Negro in American History*. New York: Putnam, 1971, p. 251.

43. Booker T. Washington. *Up From Slavery: An Autobiography*. University of Virginia Hypertext. http://xroads

.virginia.edu/~hyper/washington/ch02.html.

44. Quoted in African-American Schools of Louisa County, Virginia. www.louisaheritage.org/home.htm.

45. Quoted in Booker T. Washington. "The Wisdom & Common Sense." Booker T. Washington Society. www.btwsociety.org/library/misc/quotes.php.

46. Quoted in Louis R. Harlan, ed. *The Booker T. Washington Papers*. Vol. 3. Urbana: University of Illinois Press, 1974, p. 583.

47. Quoted in Richard Wormser. "Niagara Movement (1905–10)." *The Rise and Fall of Jim Crow*, PBS. www.pbs.org/wnet/jimcrow/stories_events_niagara.html.

## Chapter Five: The Civil Rights Movement

48. Quoted in Katy Reckdahl. "Plessy and Ferguson Unveil Plaque Today Marking Their Ancestors' Actions." *New Orleans Times-Picayune*, February 11, 2009. www.nola.com/news/index.ssf/2009/02/plessy_vs_ferguson_photo.html.

49. Quoted in Mary Maruca. Brown v. Board of Education *National Historic Site*. Tucson, AZ: Western National Parks Association, 2003. www.cr.nps.gov/history/online_books/brvb/brown.htm.

50. Quoted in Historical Marker Database. "Rosa Parks Montgomery Bus Boycott." www.hmdb.org/marker.asp?marker=28176.

51. Rosa Parks and Gregory J. Reed. *Quiet Strength: The Faith, the Hope, and the Heart of a Woman Who Changed the Nation*. Grand Rapids, MI: Zondervan, 1994, p. 26.

52. Quoted in David Jackson. "Barack Obama Sits on Rosa Parks Bus." *Detroit Free Press*, April 19, 2012. www.freep.com/article/20120419/NEWS01/120419044/Barack-Obama-sits-Rosa-Parks-bus?odyssey=tab%7Ctopnews%7Ctext%7CFRONT PAGE.

53. Quoted in Brad Norington. "Obama Sees King's Dream Set in Stone." *Australian* (Surry Hills, New South Wales), October 18, 2011, p. 12.

54. Quoted in Thomas R. Brooks. *Walls Come Tumbling Down: A History of the Civil Rights Movement, 1940–1970*. Englewood Cliffs, NJ: Prentice Hall, 1974, p. 165.

55. Quoted in August Meier, Elliot Rudwick, and John Bracey Jr., eds. *Black Protest in the Sixties: Articles from the "New York Times."* New York: Wiener, 1991, p. 40.

56. Quoted in *Encyclopedia of Alabama*. "Viola Liuzzo Memorial Marker." www.encyclopediaofalabama.org//face/Multimedia.jsp?id=m-3880.

## Chapter Six: African American Achievers

57. Phillis Wheatley. "On Being Brought from Africa to America." Poems by

Phillis Wheatley. www.vcu.edu/eng
web/webtexts/Wheatley/phil.htm.

58. Meredith Bergmann. "Boston Wom-
en's Memorial Dedication Ceremony."
City of Boston, October, 25 2003.
www.cityofboston.gov/women/MB
_speech.asp.

59. Quoted in Library of Congress.
"Today in History: November 9;
Benjamin Banneker." http://memory
.loc.gov/ammem/today/nov09.html.

60. Thomas Jefferson. "Letter to Benjamin Banneker." TeachingAmerican-
History.org. http://teachingamerican
history.org/library/index.asp?document
=458.

61. Quoted in Waymarking. "GW Carver." www.waymarking.com/gallery/
image.aspx?f=1&guid=e389839f-fa91
-418b-89ff-e25777ddbfa2.

62. Quoted in Cleveland Area History.
"Garrett Morgan, Cleveland Inven-

tor." February 1, 2010. www.cleve
landareahistory.com/2010/02/garrett
-morgan-cleveland-inventor.html.

63. Quoted in Historical Marker Database.
"Robert Johnson Birthplace." www.hm
db.org/marker.asp?marker=50874.

64. Quoted in Katrine Ames. "She Let
Freedom Sing." *Newsweek*, April 19,
1993, p. 73.

65. Quoted in Lamont H. Yeakey. "A
Student Without Peer: The Under-
graduate College Years of Paul
Robeson." *Journal of Negro Education*,
Autumn 1973. www.pages.drexel.edu
/~rosenl/sports%20Folder/Robeson
%20as%20a%20Student.pdf.

66. Quoted in Barry M. Bloom. "Baseball
Pays Tribute to Pioneer Robinson."
MLB.com, April 15, 2012. http://mlb.
mlb.com/news/article.jsp?ymd=201
20415&content_id=28741544&vkey
=news_mlb&c_id=mlb.

67. Savage. *Monument Wars*, p. 217.

# For More Information

## Books

Kirk Savage. *Standing Soldiers, Kneeling Slaves: Race, War, and Monument in Nineteenth-Century America.* Princeton, NJ: Princeton University Press, 1997. The author discusses how monuments built after the Civil War prompted a philosophical battle involving issues from both the war and race.

Kirk Savage. *Monument Wars: Washington, D.C., the National Mall, and the Transformation of the Memorial Landscape.* Berkeley: University of California Press, 2005. Savage details the history of monuments in the nation's capital, including how ideas about monuments have changed.

## Websites

**Bench by the Road Project** (www.toni morrisonsociety.org/bench.html). The Toni Morrison Society site sponsors this project to have benches placed in honor of the famed writer to remember African American slaves.

**Freedmen's Memorial Monument to Abraham Lincoln** (www.hmdb.org /marker.asp?marker=41617). This Historical Marker Database site has pictures and information on the memorial to Abraham Lincoln that was paid for by freed slaves.

**Historical Marker Database** (www.hm db.org). A comprehensive and searchable online catalogue of historical sites and markers.

**Lincoln Memorial** (www.nps.gov/linc /index.htm). This National Park Service site has pictures and articles about the most prestigious memorial to Abraham Lincoln.

**Martin Luther King, Jr., National Memorial** (www.mlkmemorial.org). The site for the memorial in Washington, D.C., honoring King.

**Monuments About Slavery & Emancipation** (http://peace.maripo.com/p _slavery.htm). This comprehensive site has links to many monuments connected with African American history.

**Monuments to the United States Colored Troops (USCT)** (http://jubiloe-mancipationcentury.wordpress.com /2011/05/30/monuments-to-the-united -states-colored-troops-usct-the-list). A list of many landmarks honoring African Americans who fought in the Civil War.

**National Historic Landmarks Program** (www.nps.gov/nhl/designations/listso fnhls.htm). The National Park Service list and Internet connections to National Historic Landmarks.

**National Register of Historic Places** (www.nps.gov/nr). The main National Park Service site on historic places.

**Smithsonian National Museum of African American History and Culture** (http://nmaahc.si.edu ). The site has photographs and historic details about African American history.

**South Carolina African American Monument** (www.usca.edu/aasc /african-americanmonument.htm). This University of South Carolina site has information and pictures of this historical monument to blacks.

**Underground Railroad** (http://education .nationalgeographic.com/education /multimedia/interactive/the-under ground-railroad/?ar_a=1). This interactive National Geographic site has maps, information, photographs, and videos about how the Underground Railroad helped African Americans escape slavery.

# Index

# Picture Credits

Cover: © Edwin Remsberg/Alamy.
  © Seqoya/Shutterstock.com

© Andre Jenny/Alamy, 82

© Ann Hermes/The Christian Science
  Moitor via Getty Images, 74

© AP Images/Bill Haber, 65

© AP Images/Bob Child, 26

© AP Images/Bruce Smith, 29, 31

© AP Images/Columbus Dispatch, Renee
  Sauer, 33

© AP Images/Kathleen Lange, 52

© AP Images/The Newport News Daily
  press, Buddy Norris, 43

© AP Images/News & Record, Lynn
  Hey, 73

© AP Images/Rex Features via AP
  Images, 8

© AP Images/The Virginia-Pilot, L. Todd
  Spencer, 45

© Carol M. Highsmith/Buyenlarge/Getty
  Images, 48

© Chip Somodevilla/Getty Images, 22

© Corbis, 20

©culliganphoto/Alamy, 19

© David Coleman/Alamy, 71

© DIZ Muenchen GmbH, Sueddeutsche
  Zeitung Photo/Alamy, 87

© Don Smetzer/Alamy, 40

© Everett Collection, Inc./Alamy, 54,
  59

© Frank Vetere/Alamy, 46

© Gary Cook/Alamy, 11

© James P. Blair/Corbis, 35

© Jim Mooney/NY Daily News Archive
  via Getty Images, 84

© John Elk III/Alamy, 39

© Michael DeFreitas North America/
  Alamy, 66

© M. Timothy O'Keefe/Alamy, 12

© Pete Souza/UPI/Landov, 68

© Phillip Louis/Alamy, 36

© Randy Duchaine/Alamy, 79

© Rich Pilling/MLB Photos via Getty
  Images, 90

© Robert Quinlan/Alamy, 16

© Sherab/Alamy, 76

© Stephen Saks Photography/Alamy,
  57, 61

© Terese Loeb Kreuzer/Alamy, 15

© Vespasian/Alamy, 86

© Yakoniva/Alamy, 63

# About the Author

Michael V. Uschan has written nearly ninety books, including *Life of an American Soldier in Iraq*, for which he won the 2005 Council for Wisconsin Writers Juvenile Nonfiction Award. It was the second time he won the award. Uschan began his career as a writer and editor with United Press International, a wire service that provided stories to newspapers, radio, and television. Journalism is sometimes called "history in a hurry." Uschan considers writing history books a natural extension of the skills he developed in his many years as a journalist. He and his wife, Barbara, reside in the Milwaukee suburb of Franklin, Wisconsin.